TANGLED ADVENTURES FOR ADULTS

MAZES LABYRINTHS

ActivityCrusades

Published by Speedy Publishing Canada Limited

ActivityCrusades
activity books

1

2

3

4

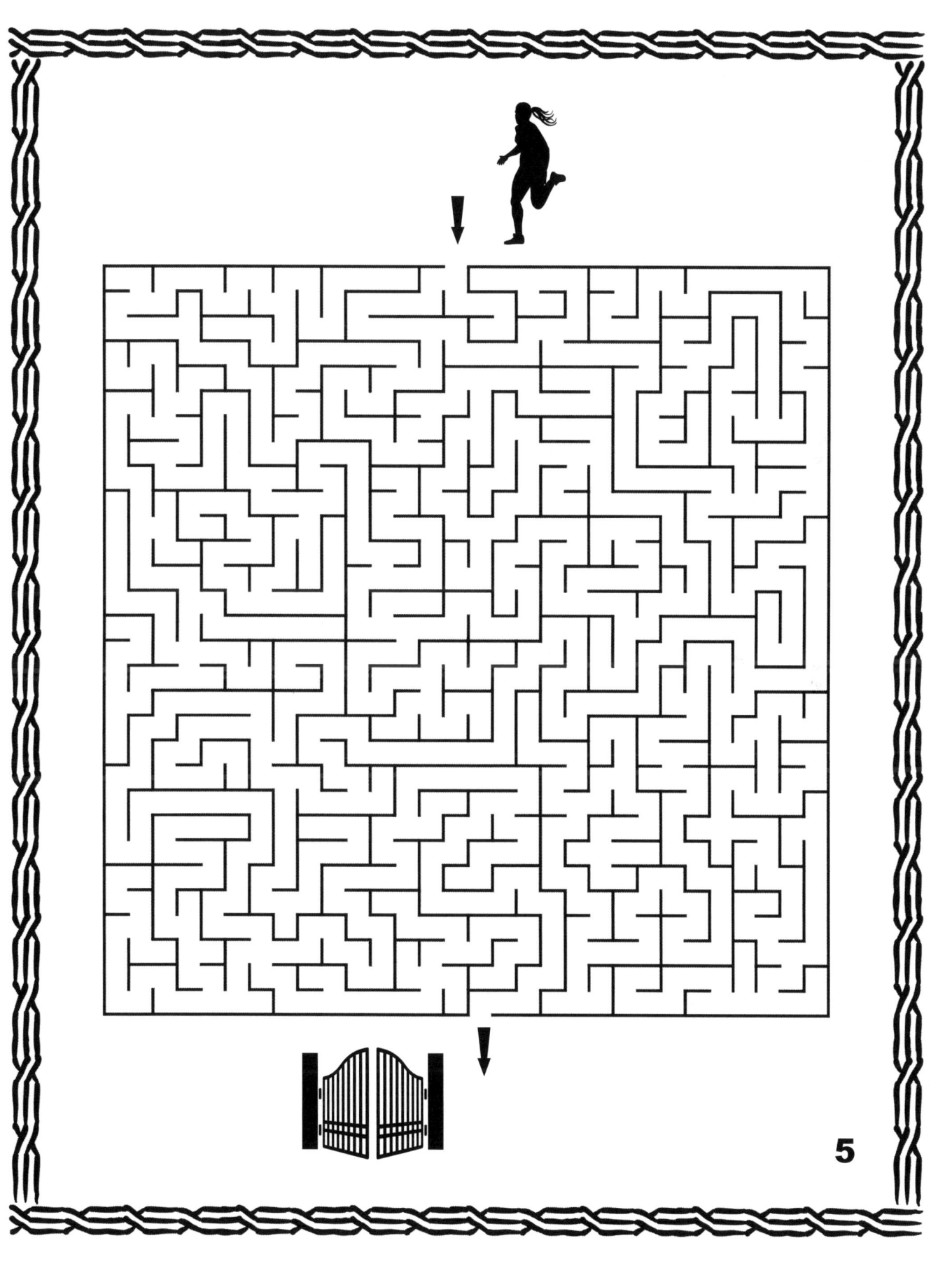

5

6

8

9

10

12

13

14

15

16

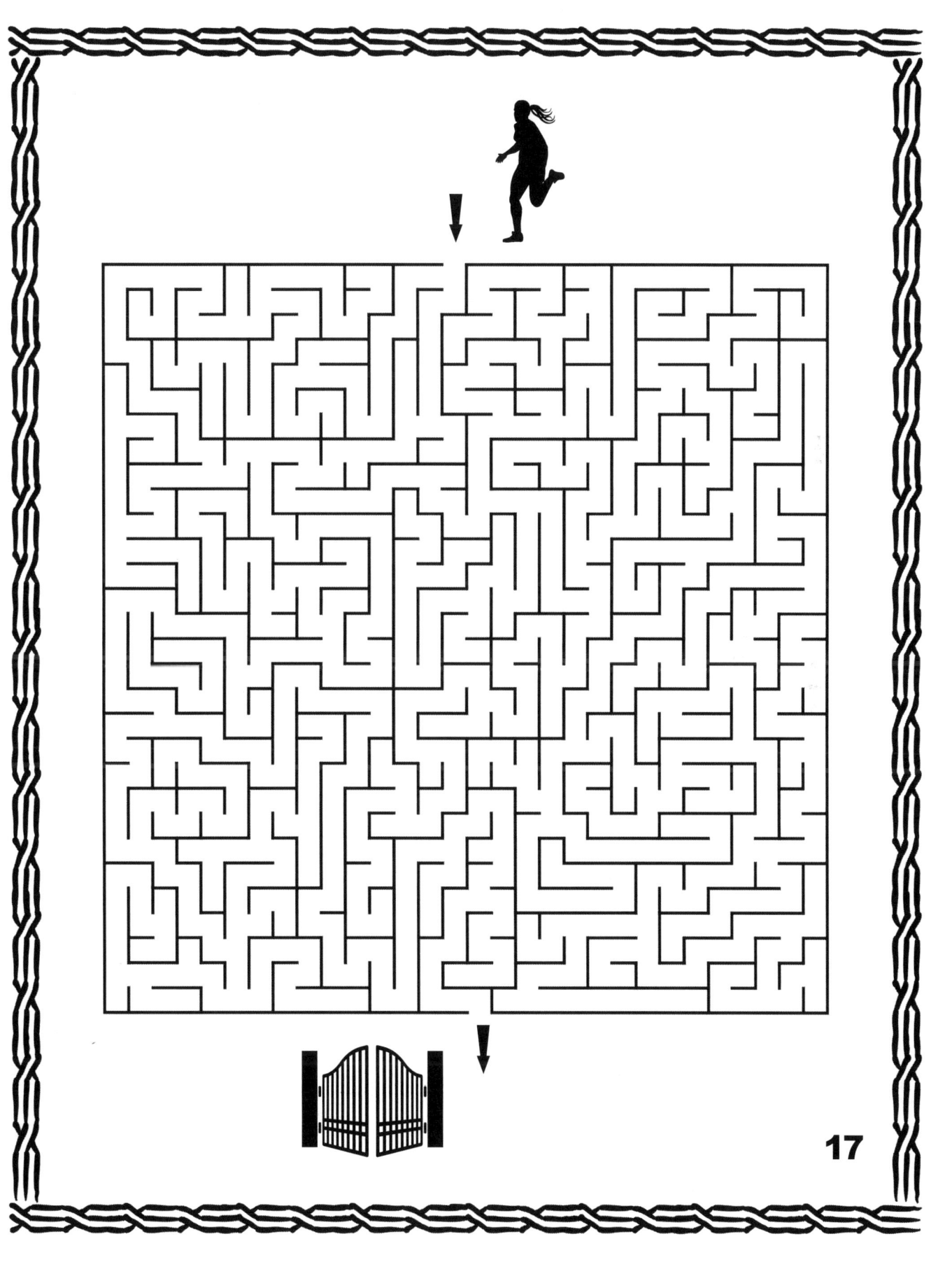

20

21

23

24

25

26

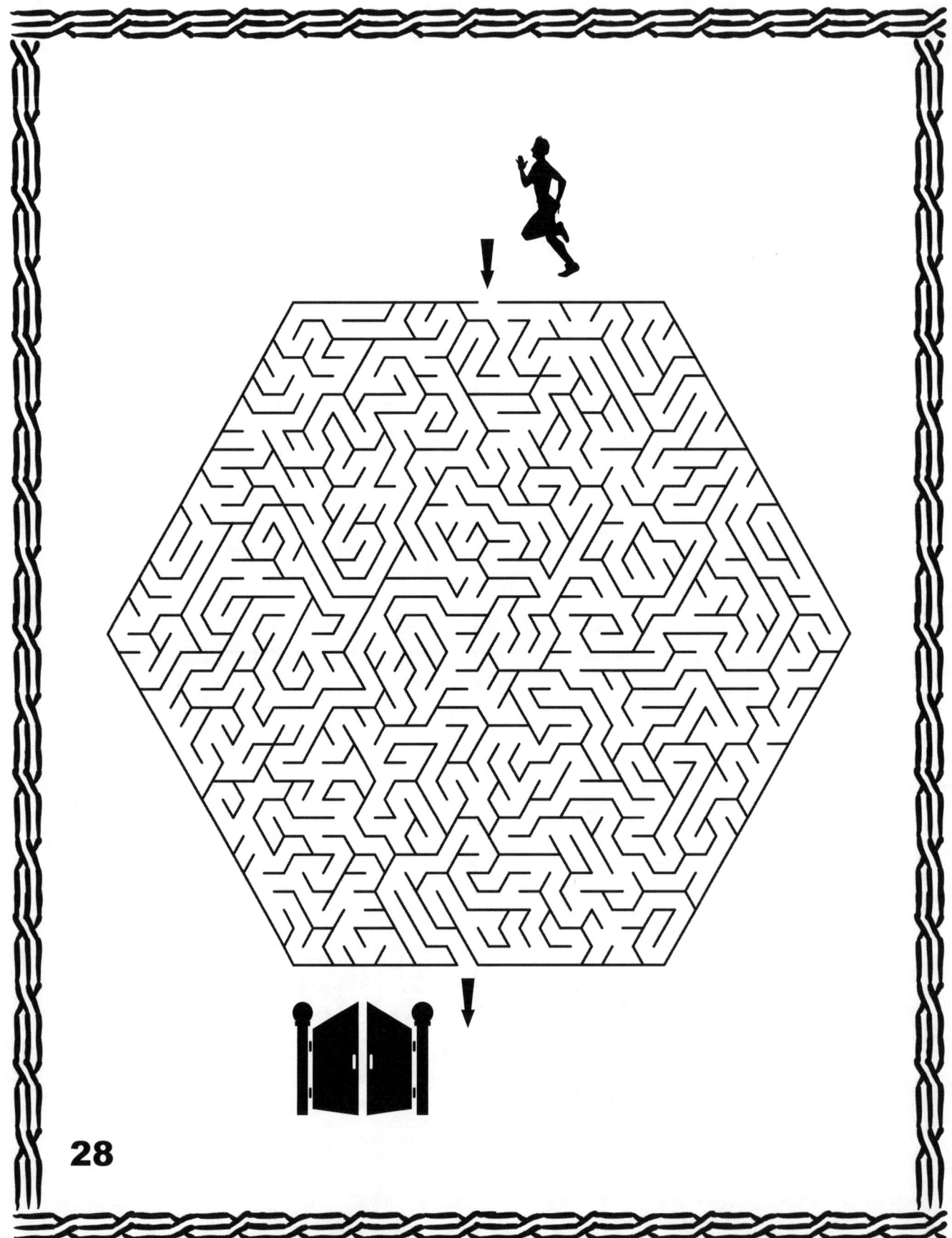

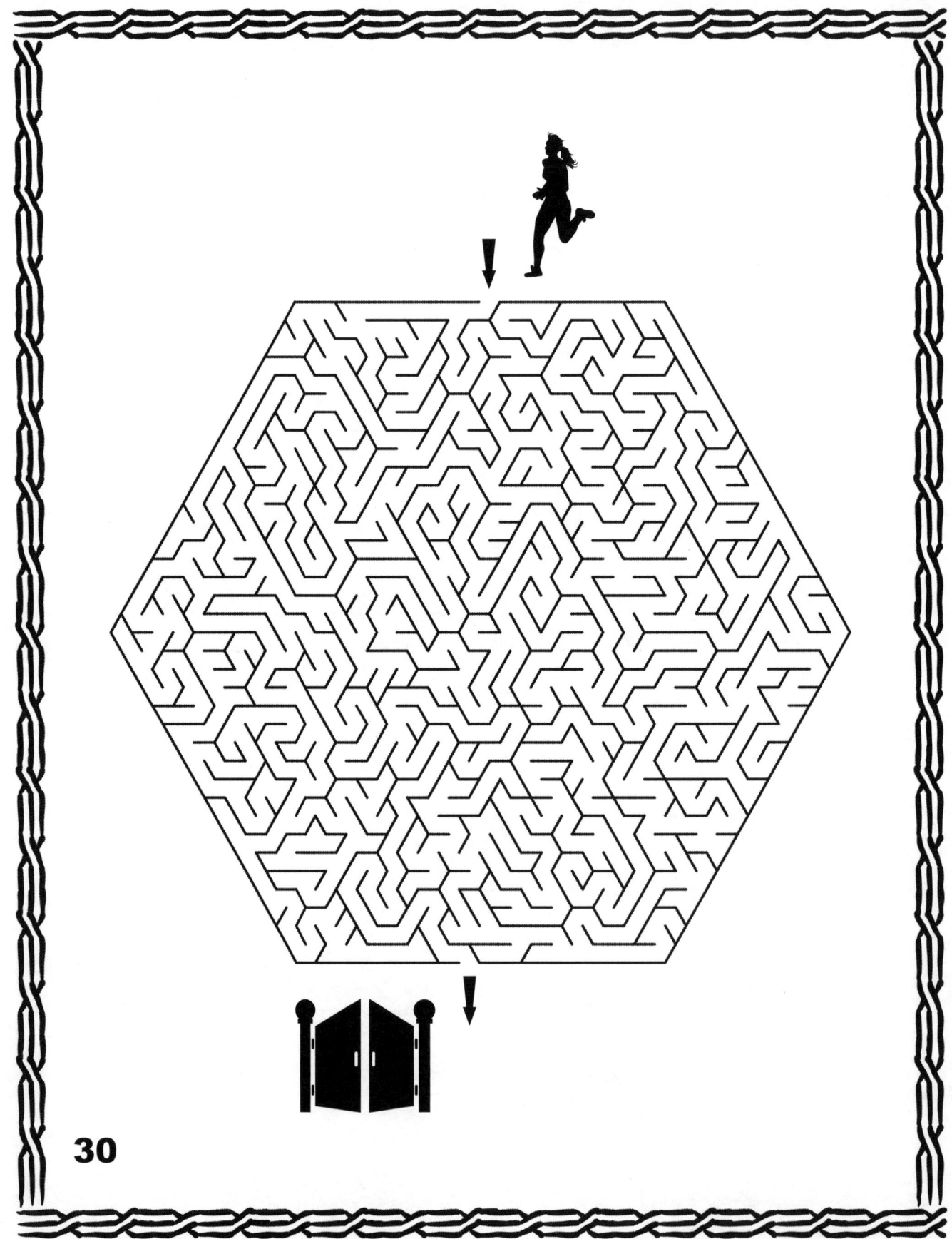

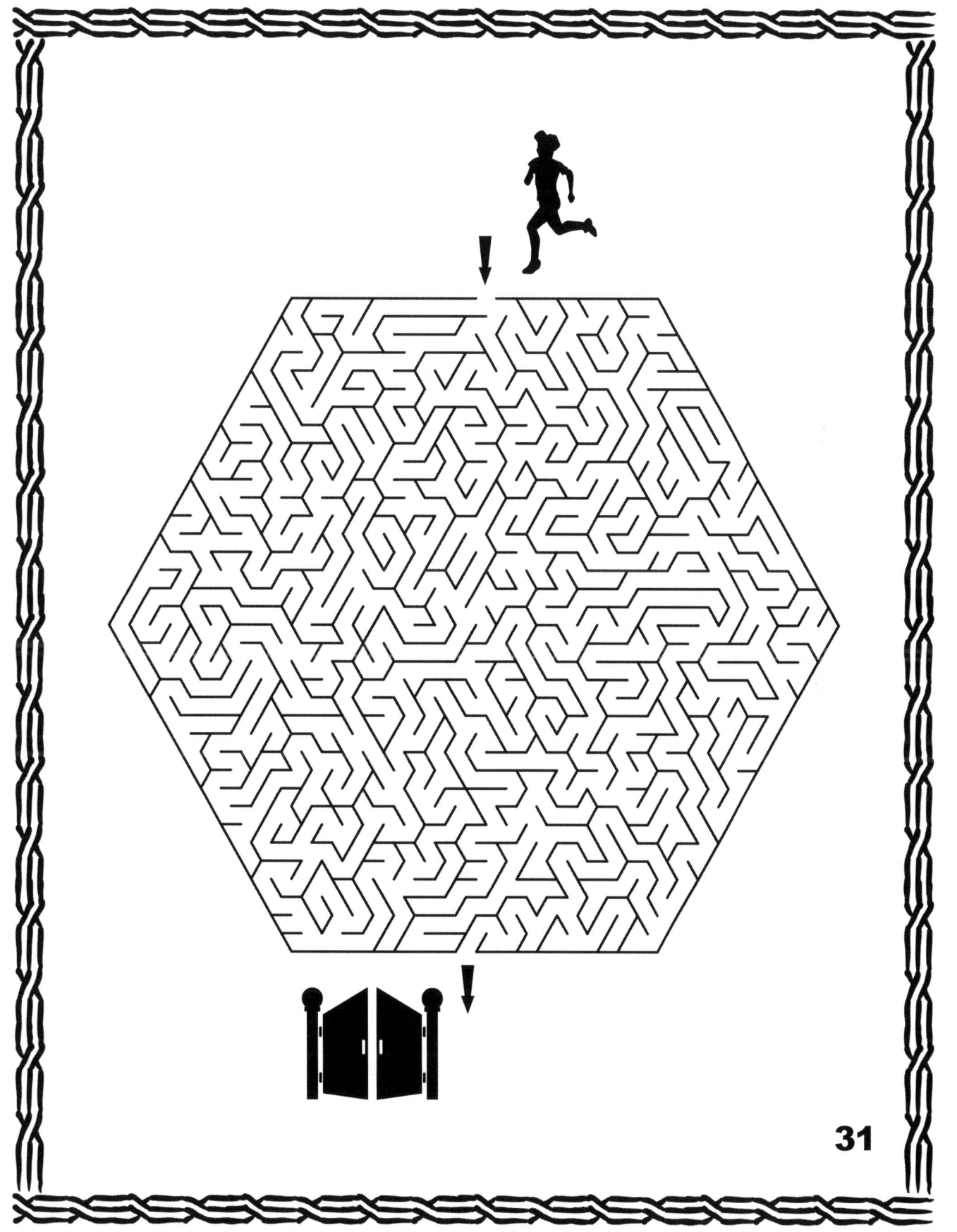

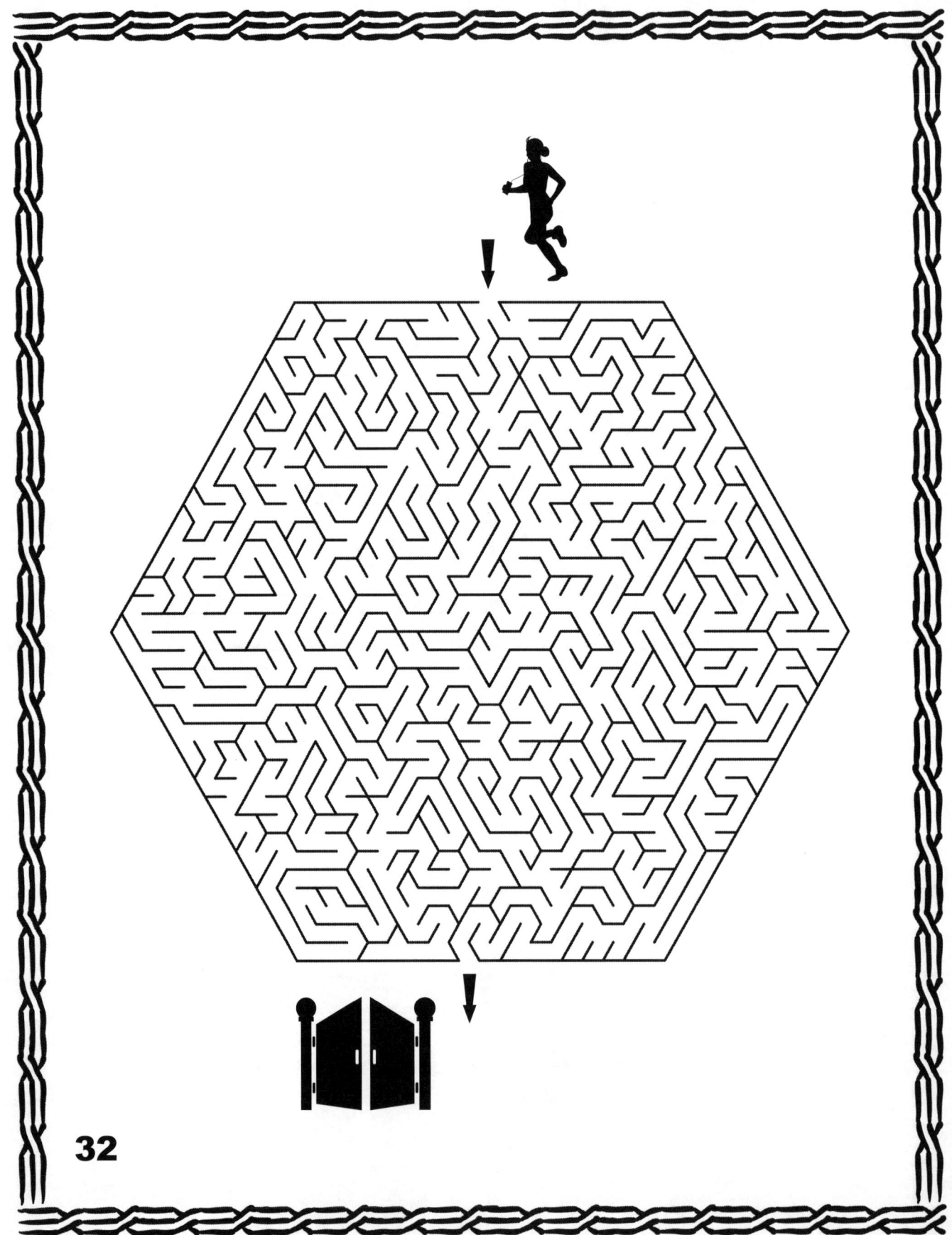

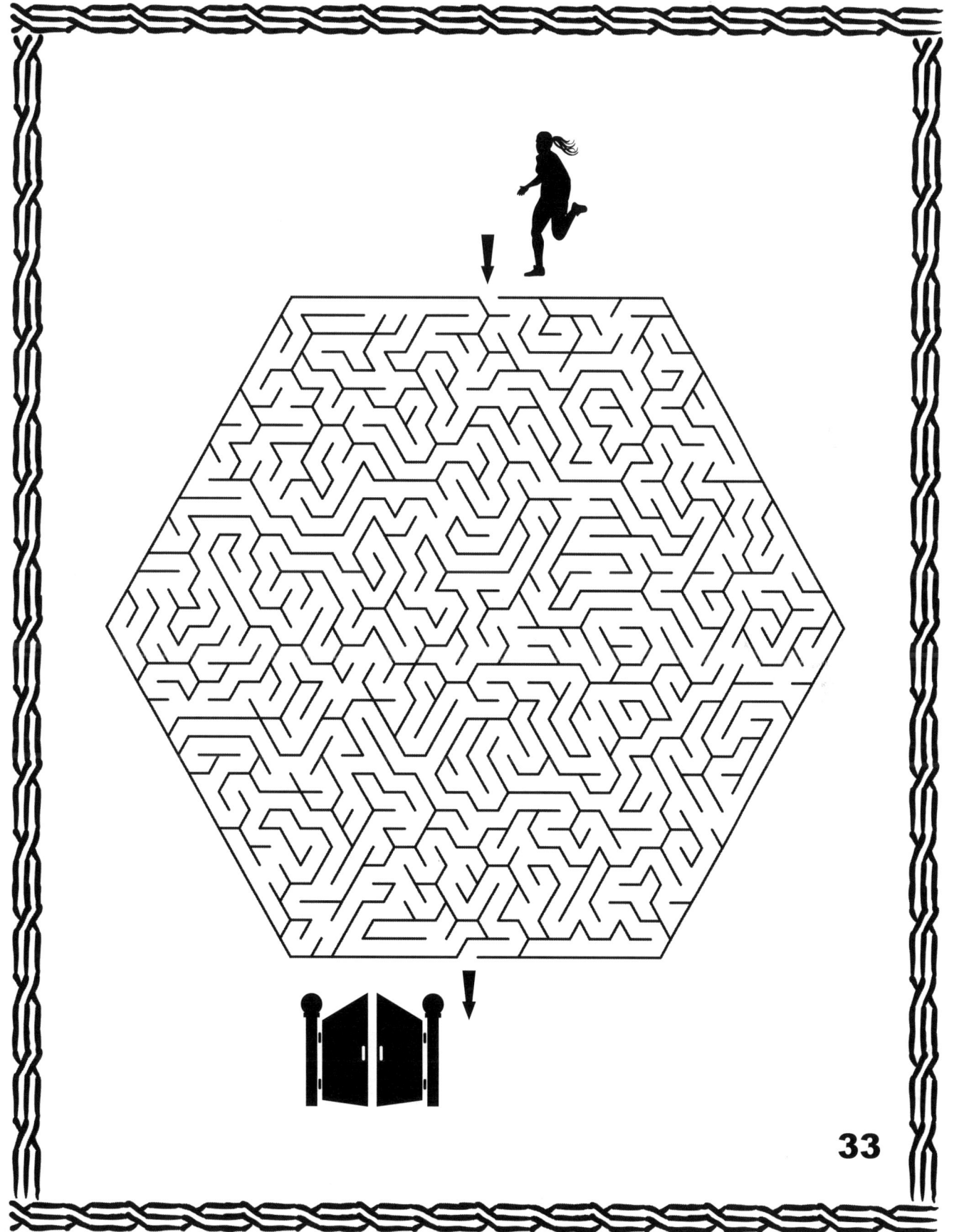

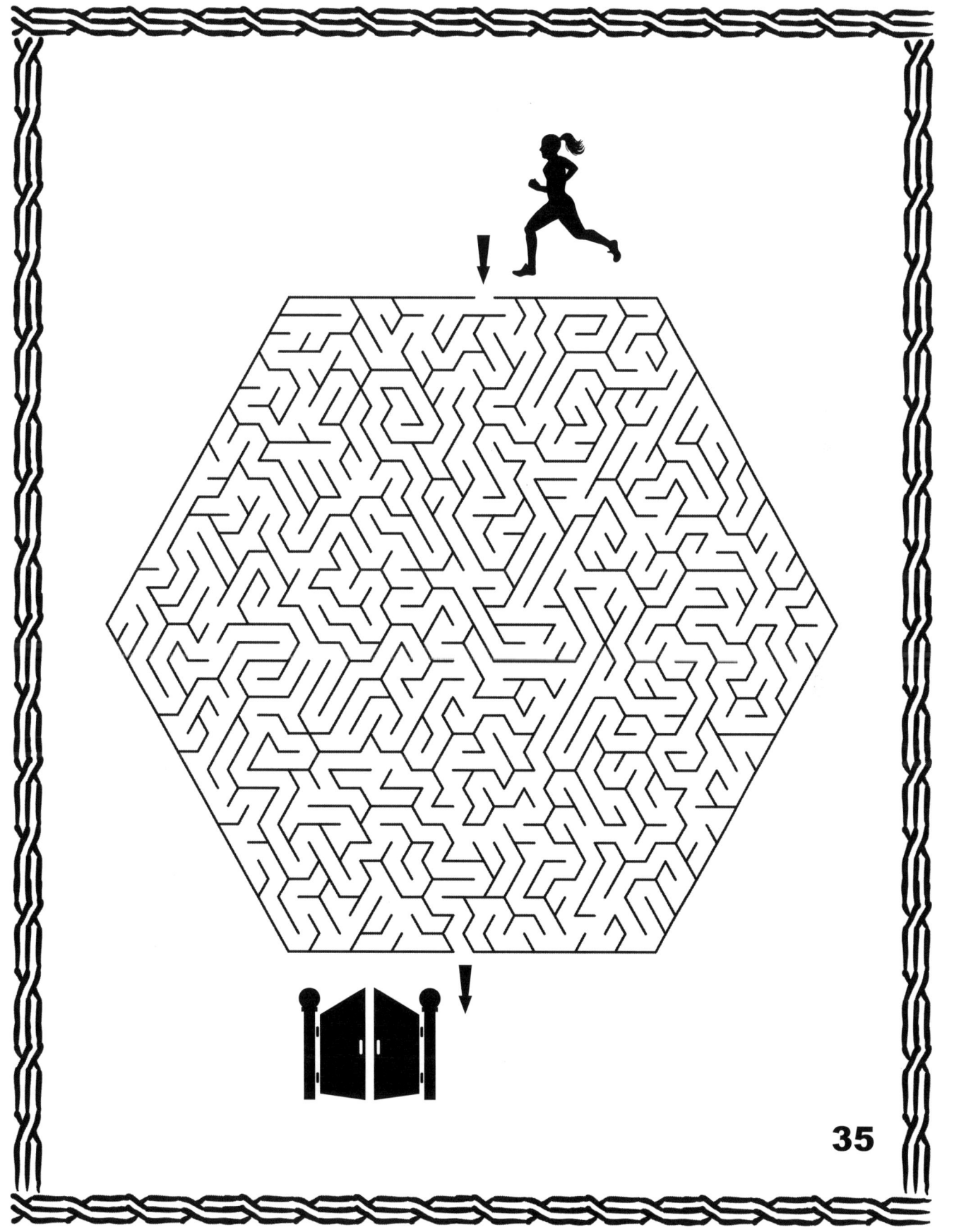

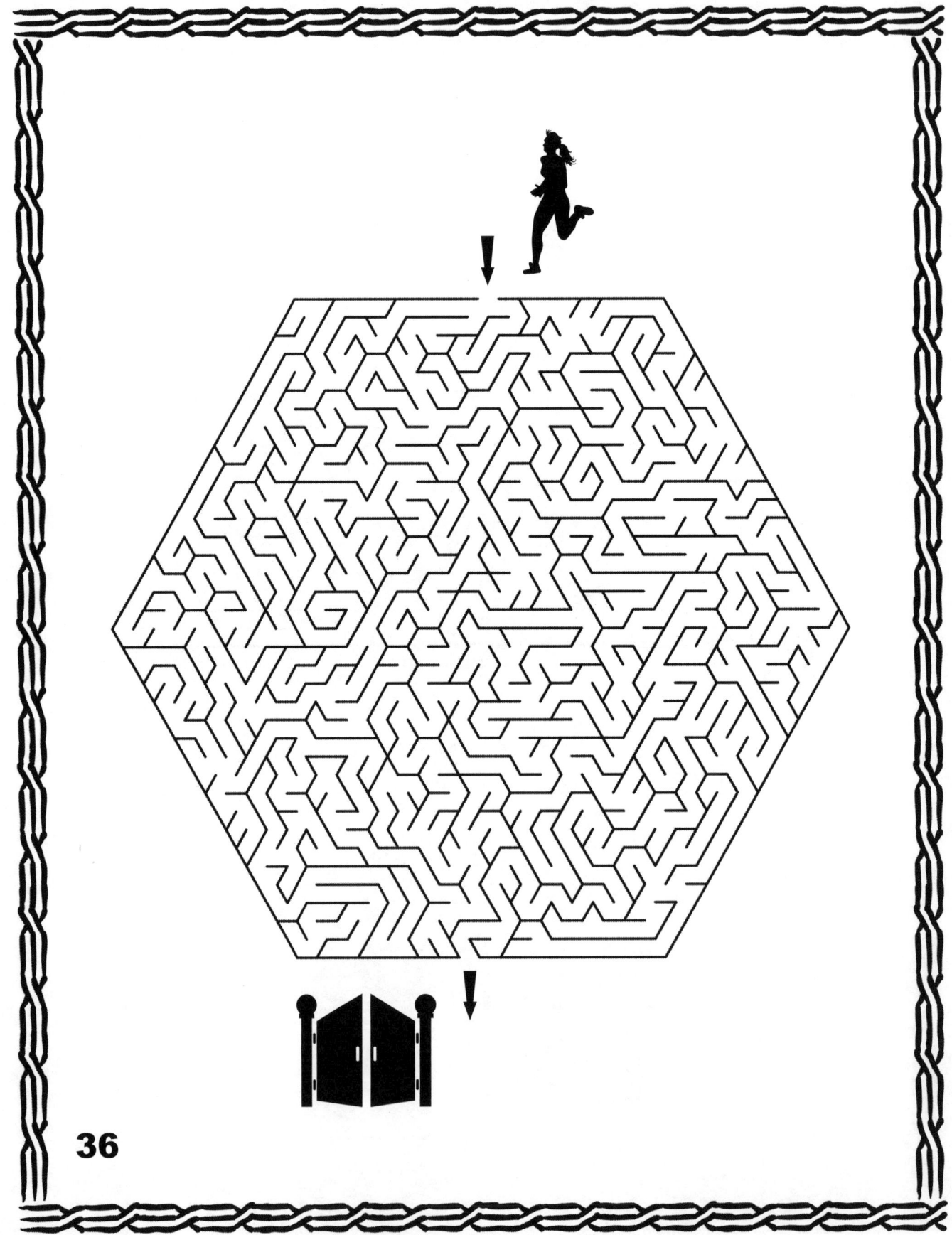

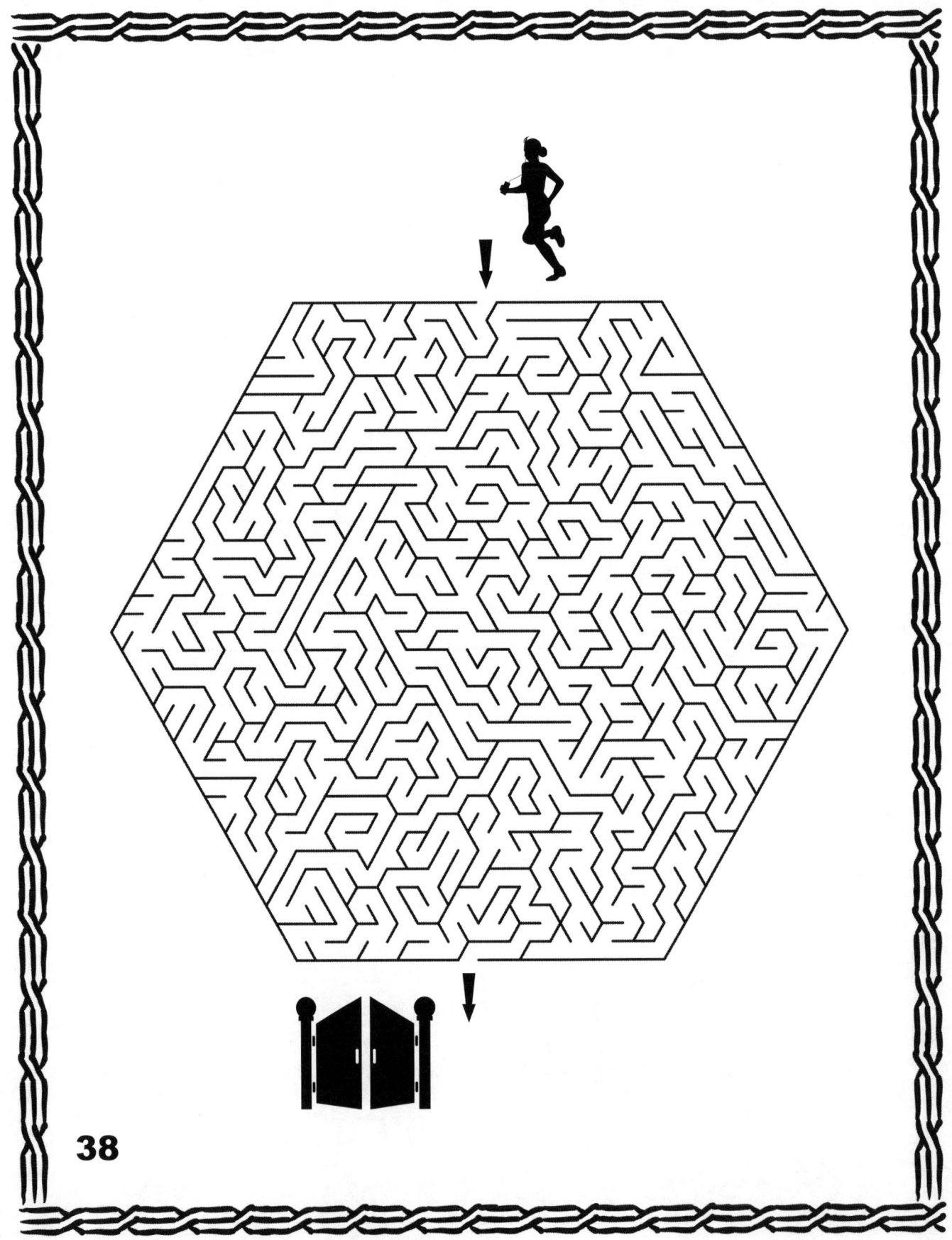

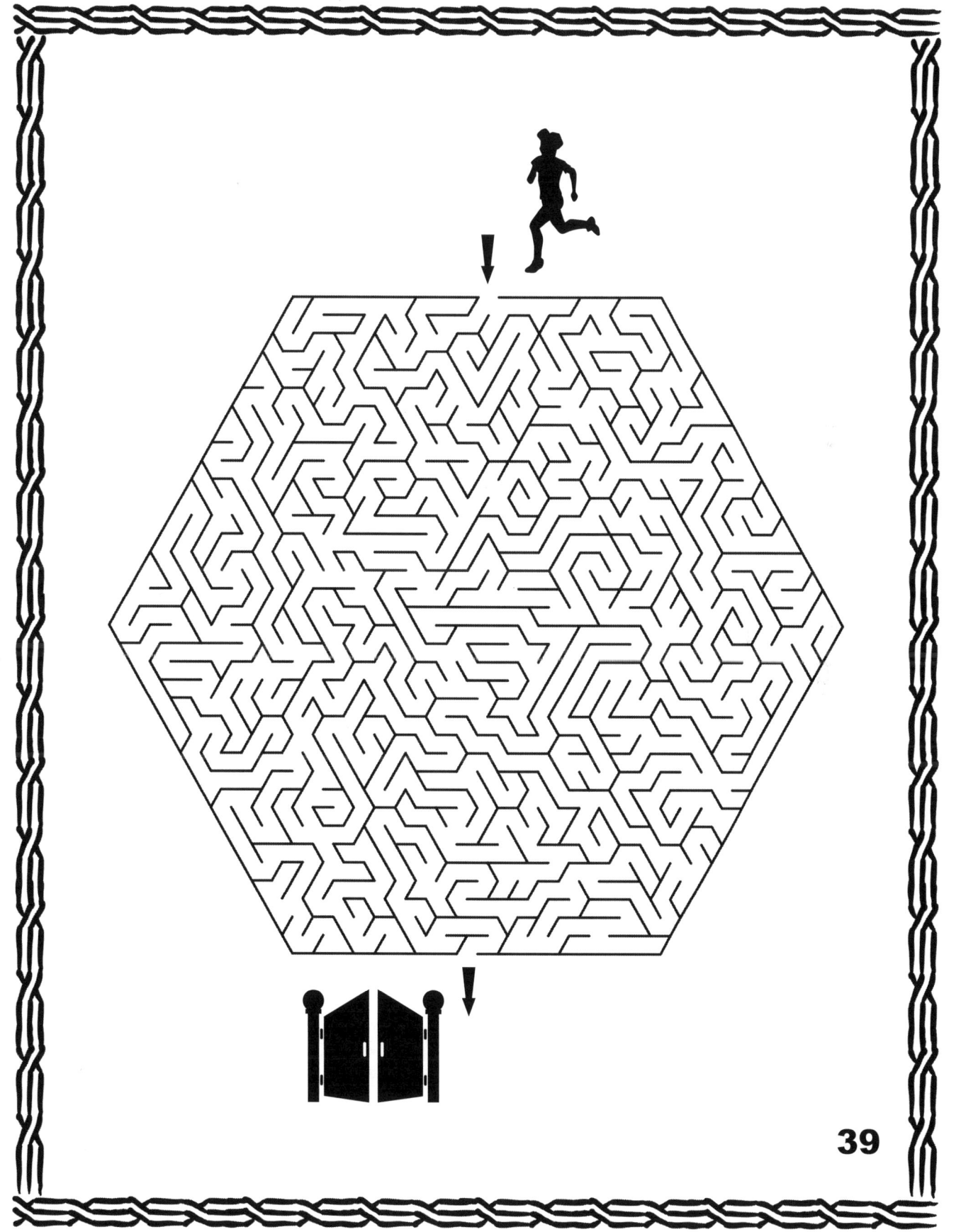

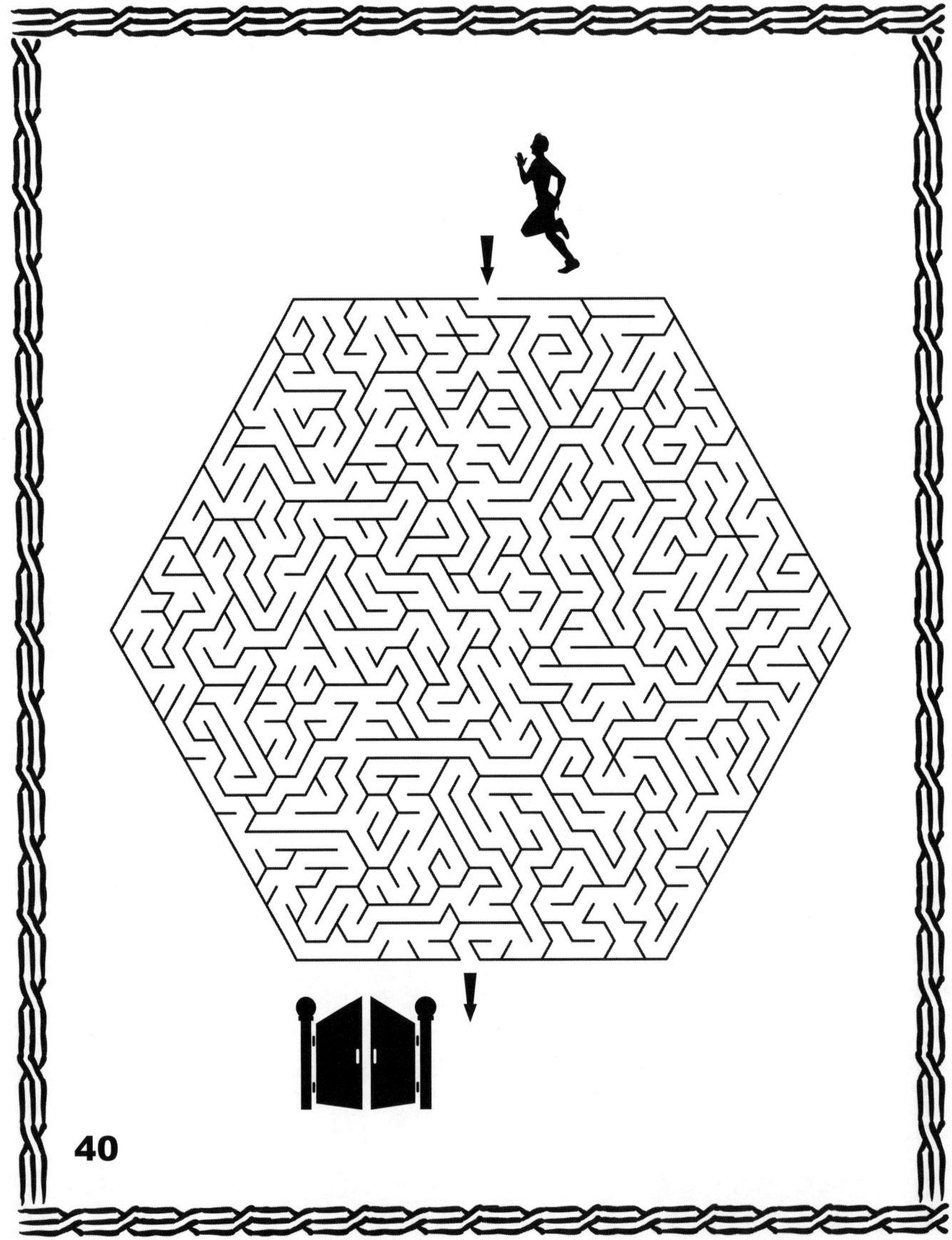

40

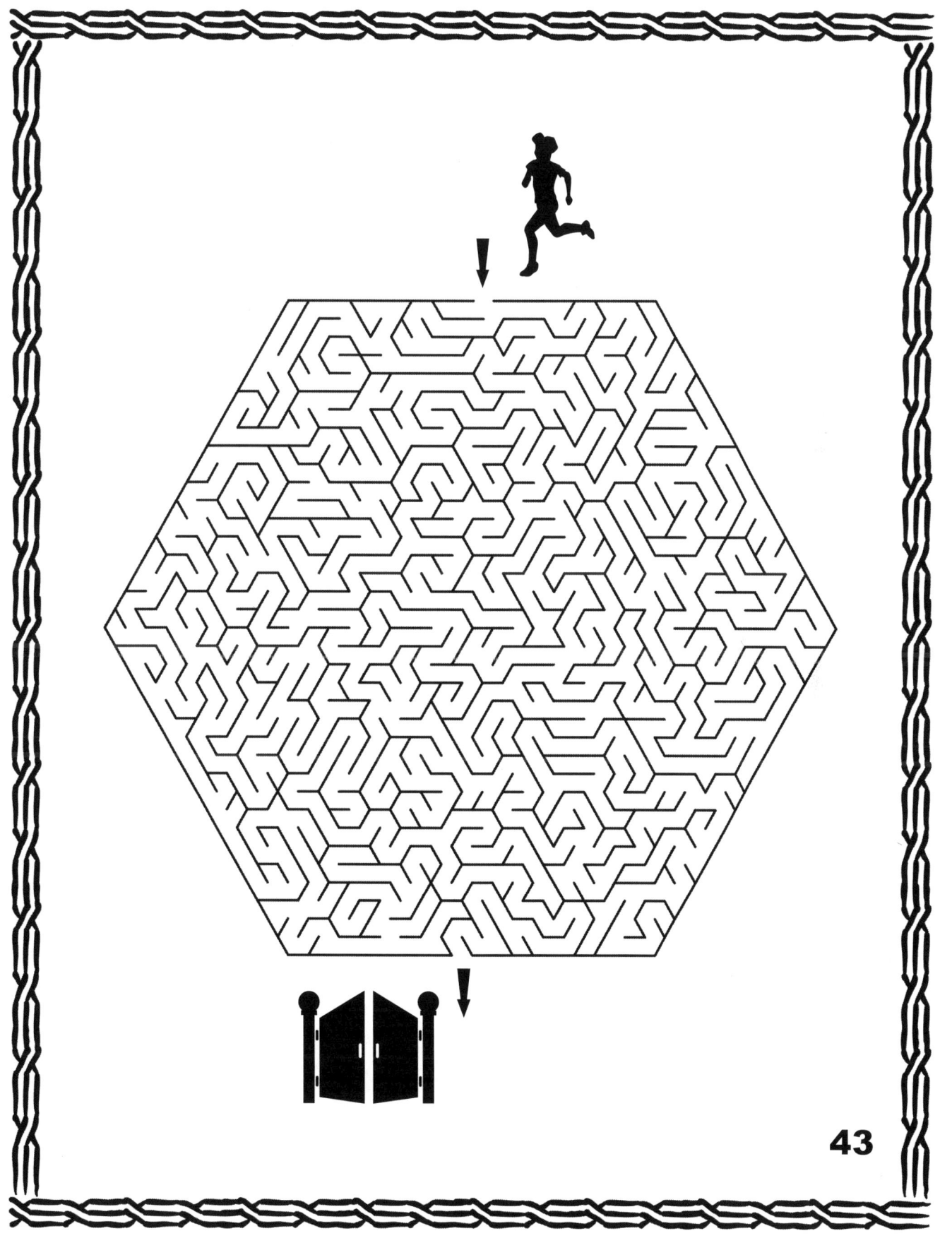

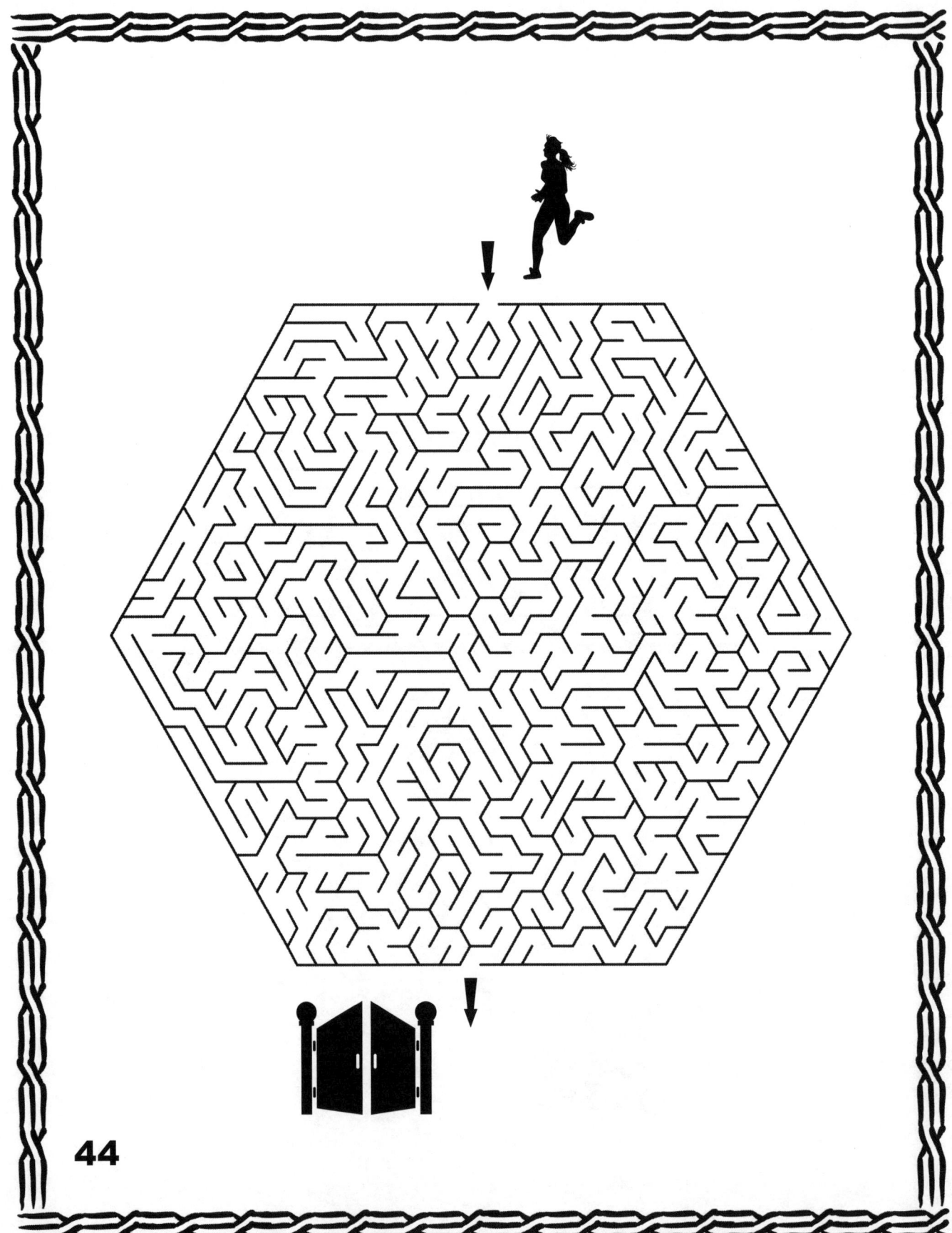

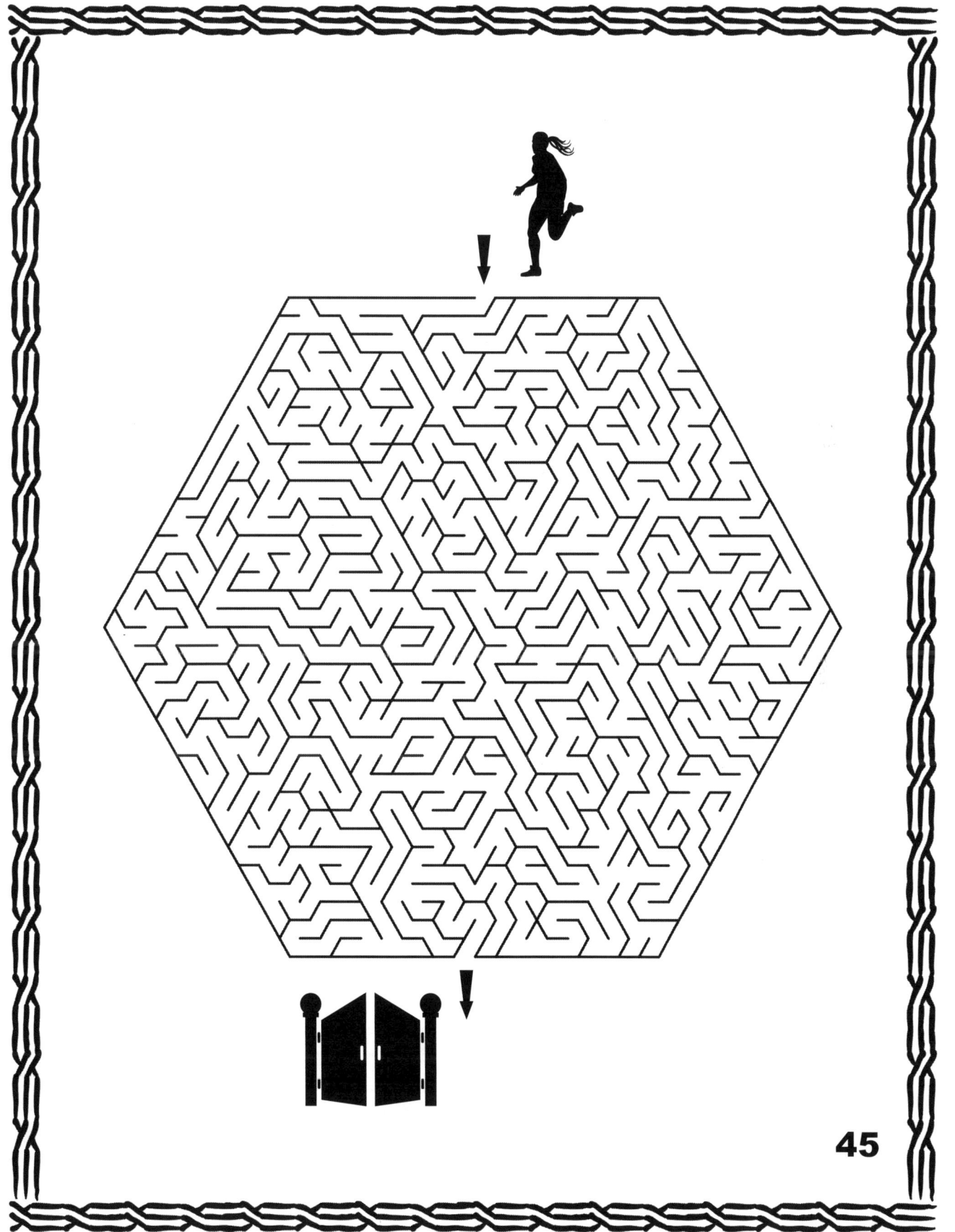

45

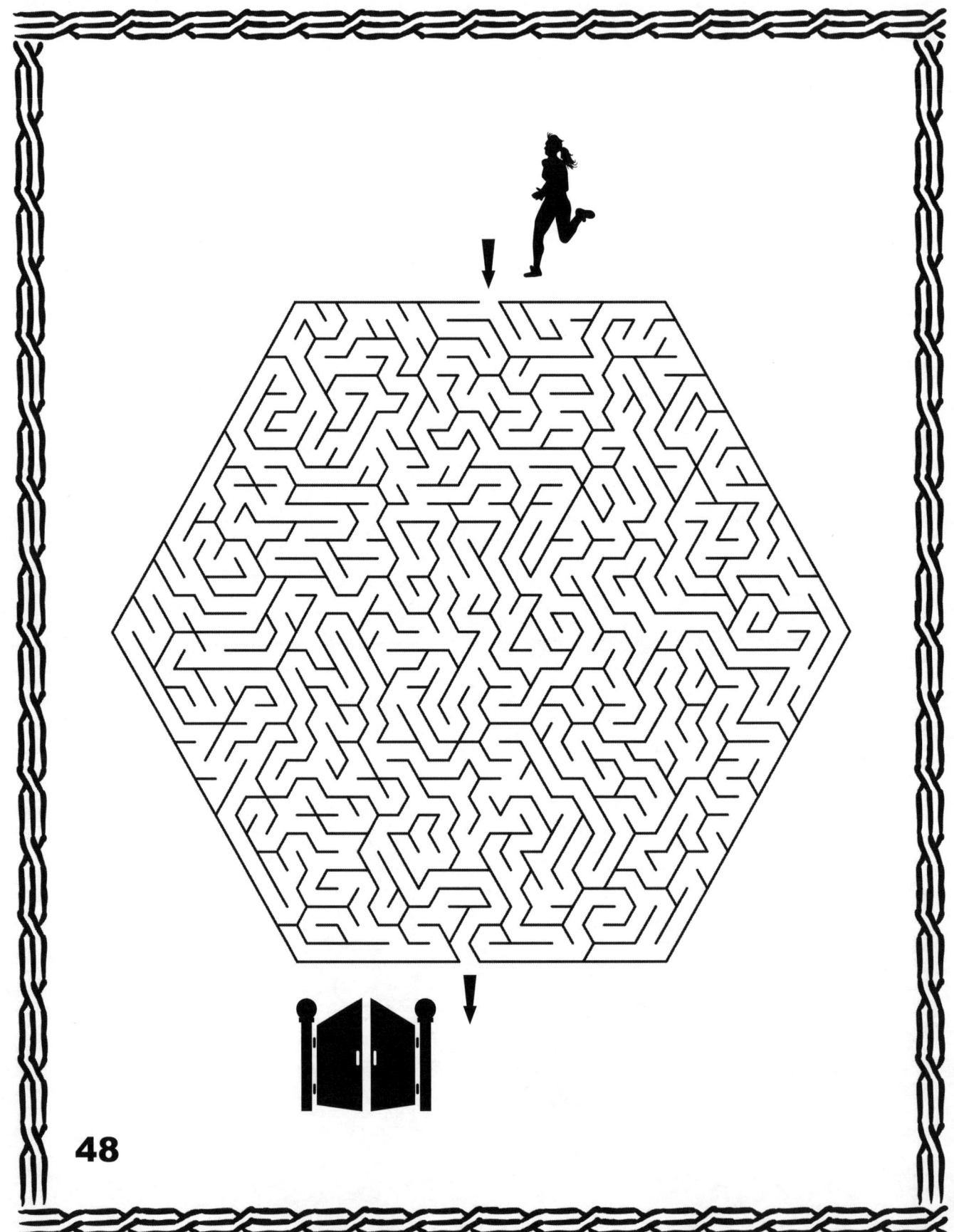

48

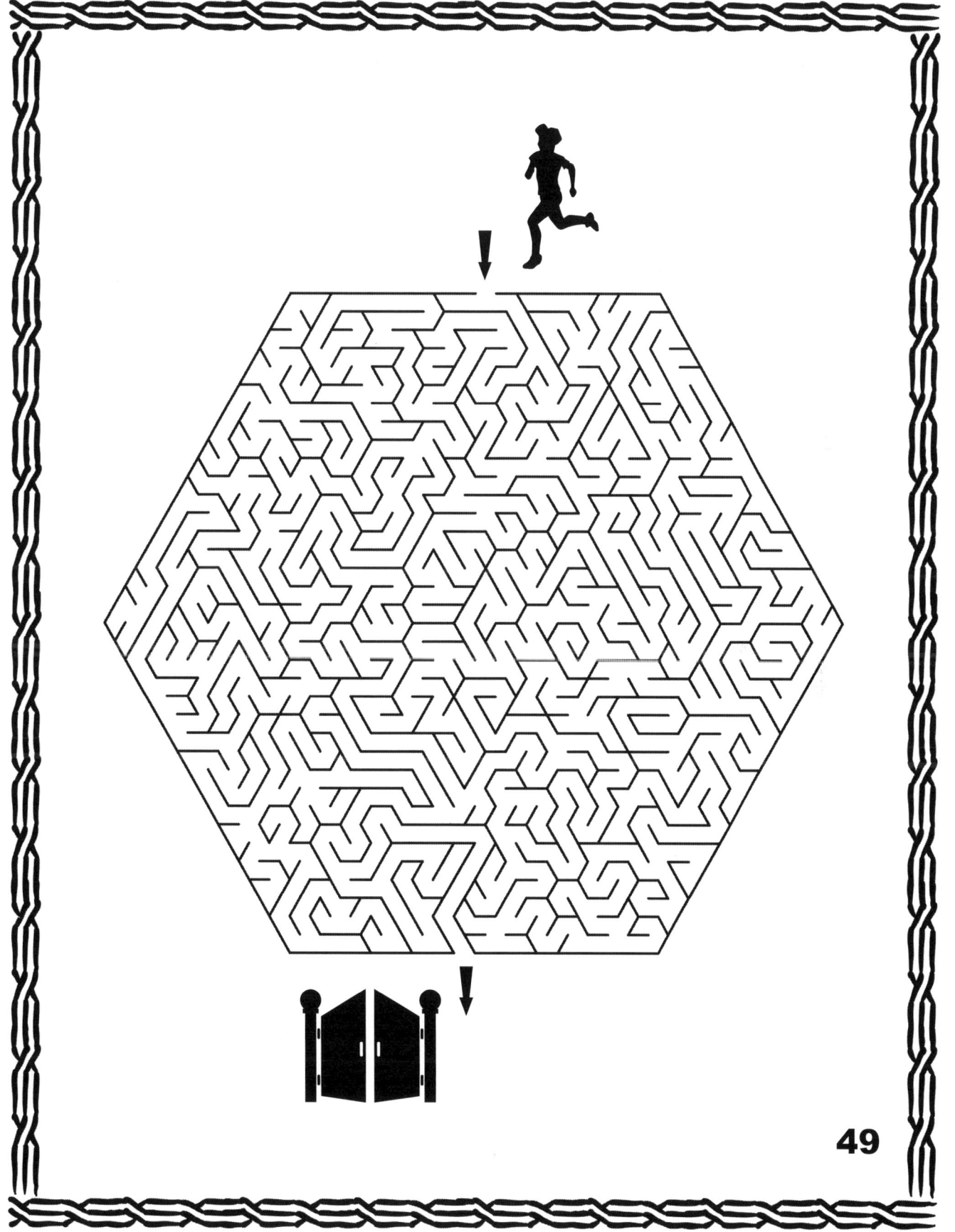

49

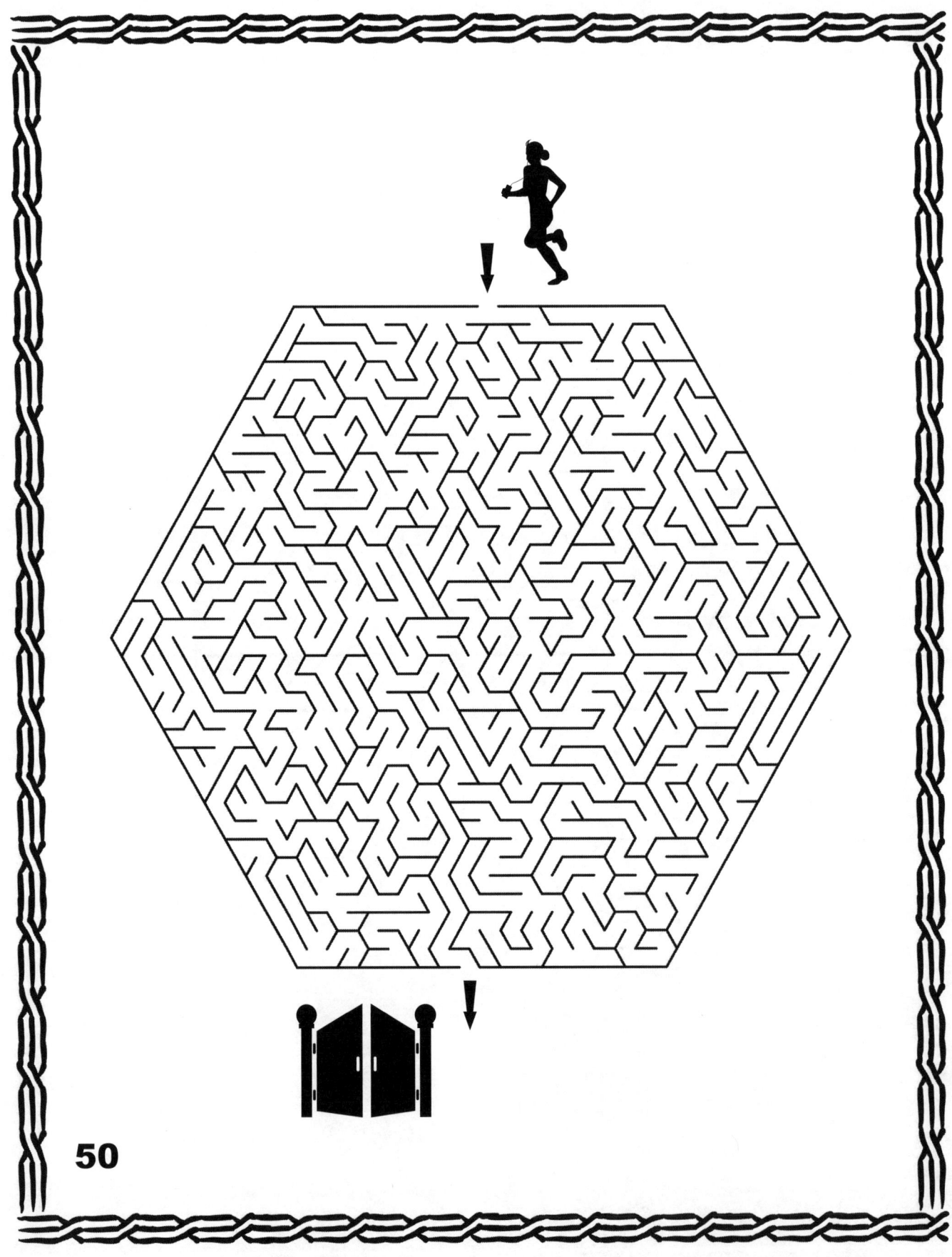

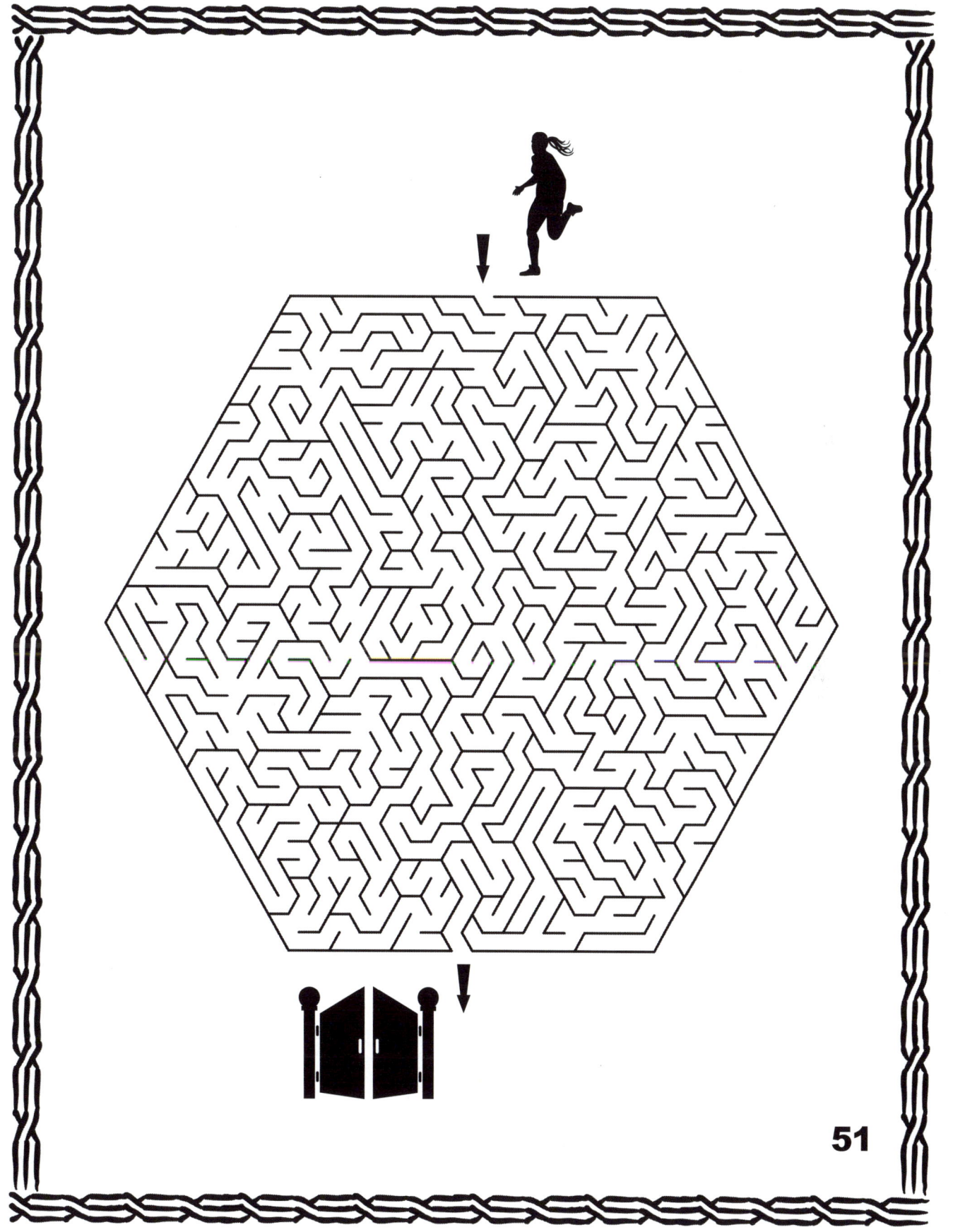

54

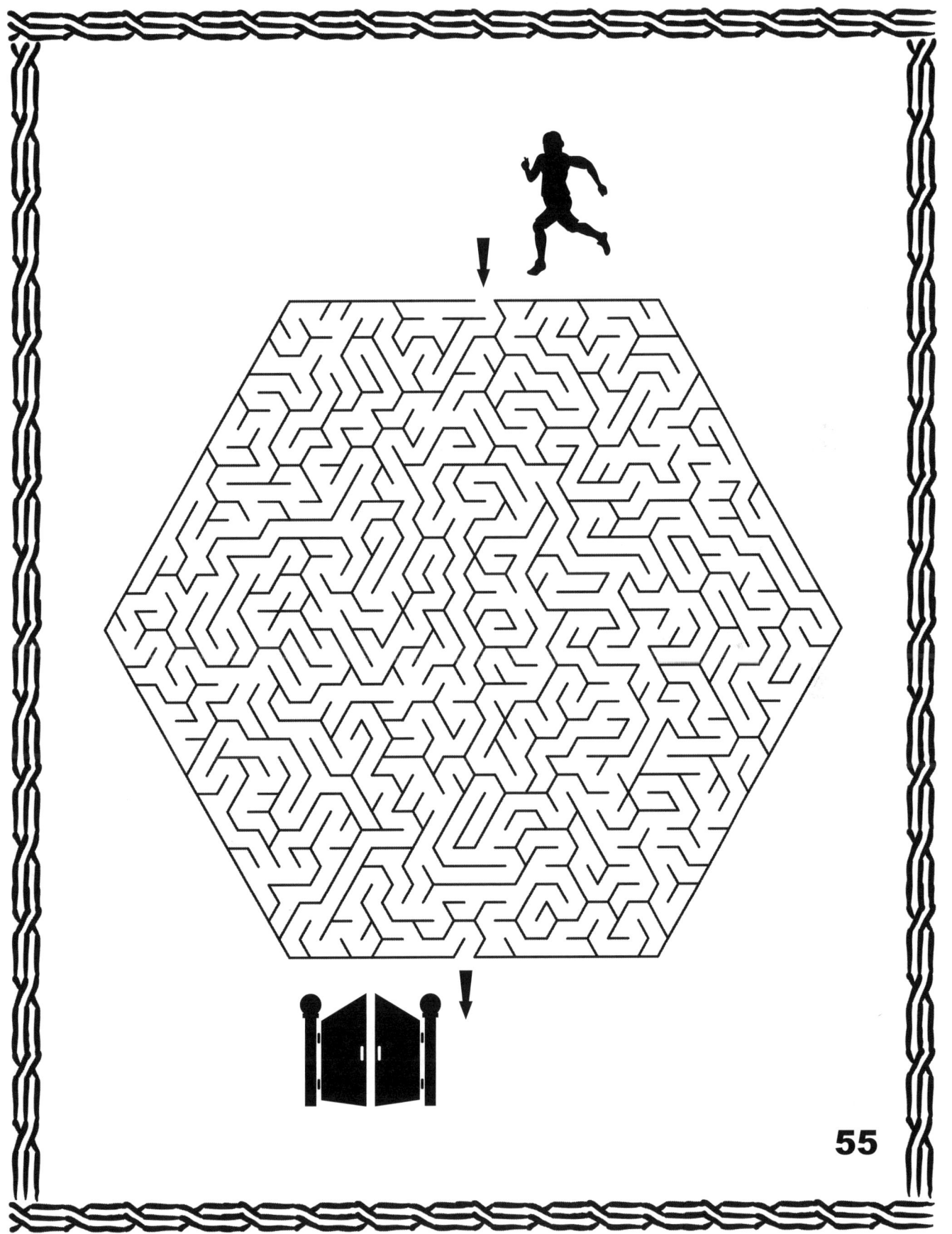

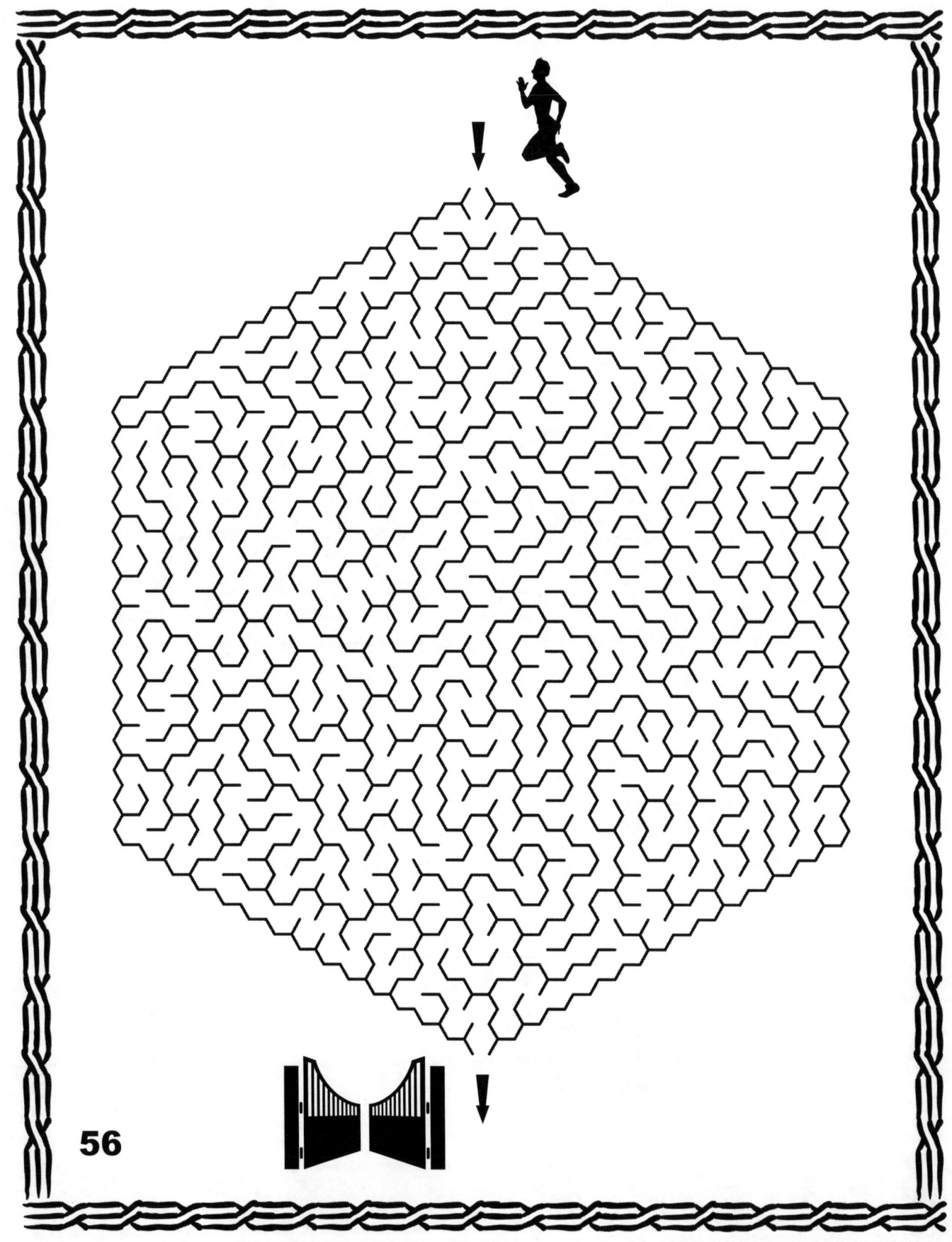

56

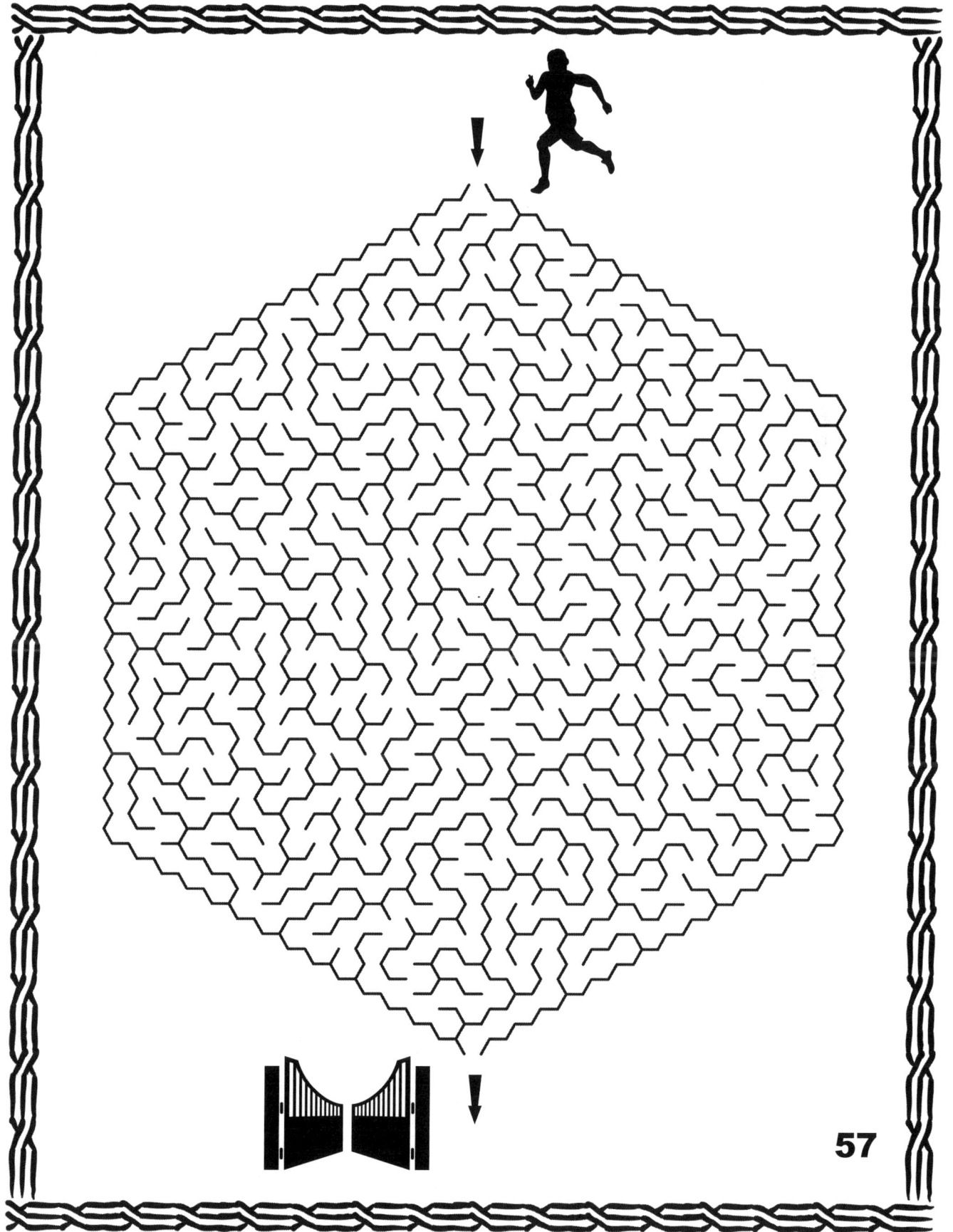

57

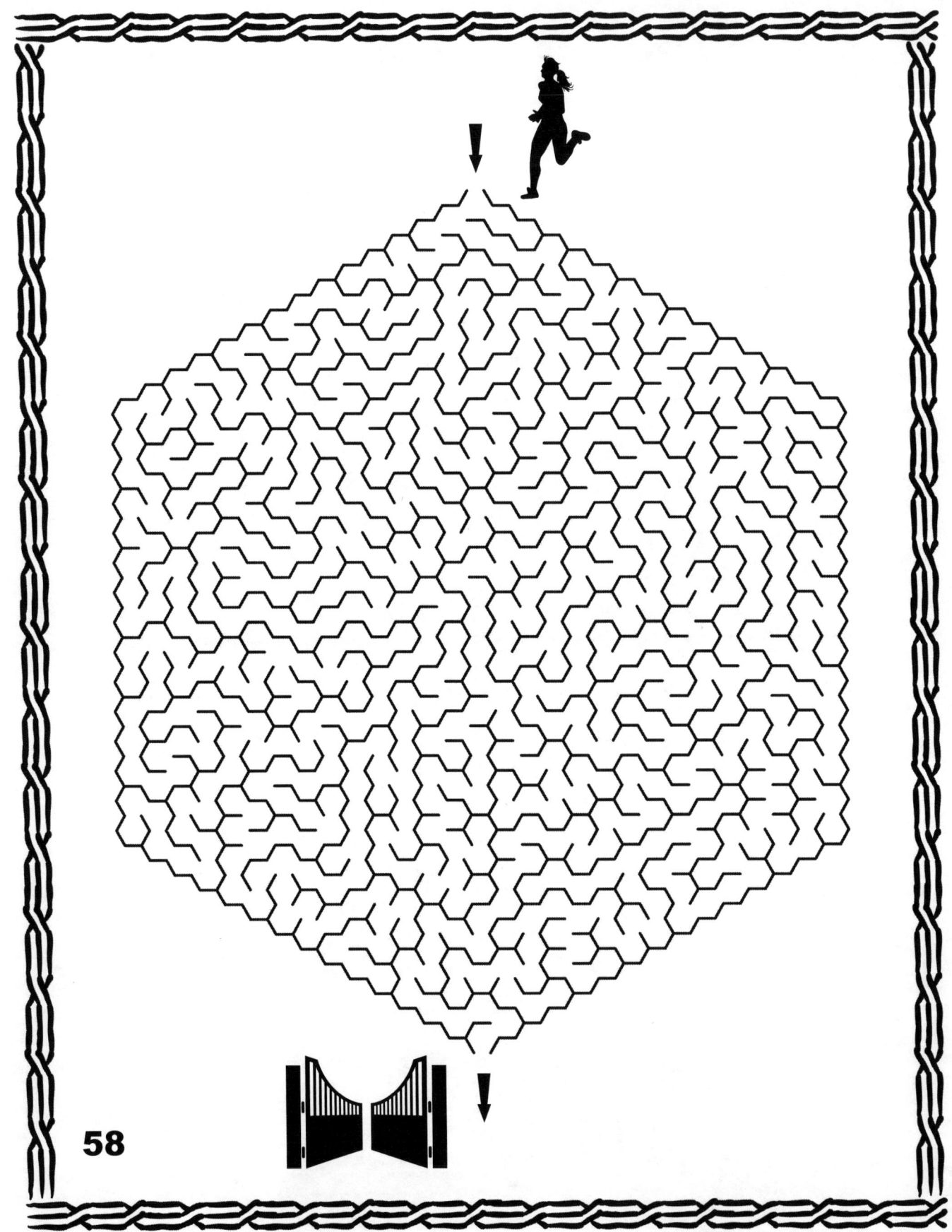

58

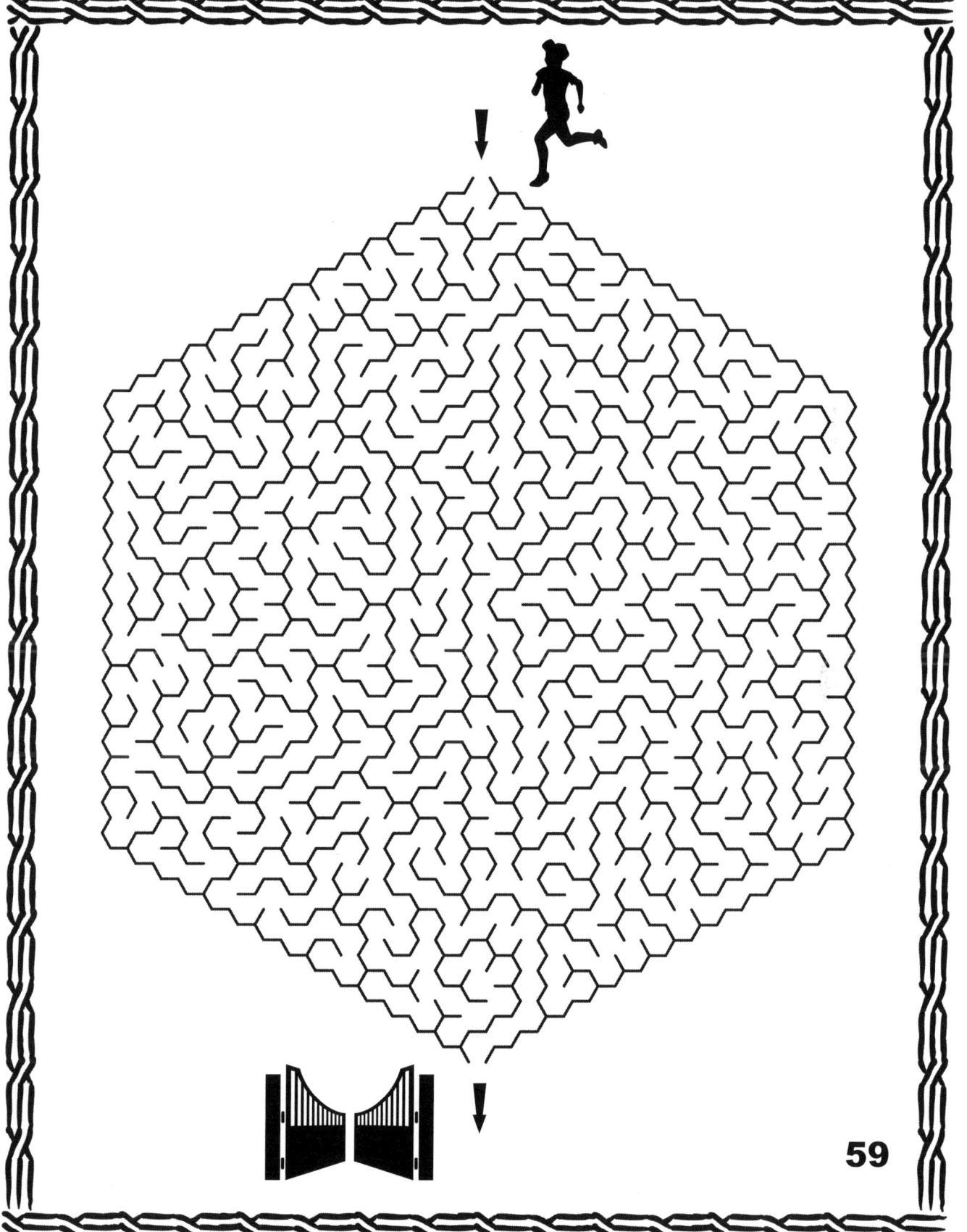

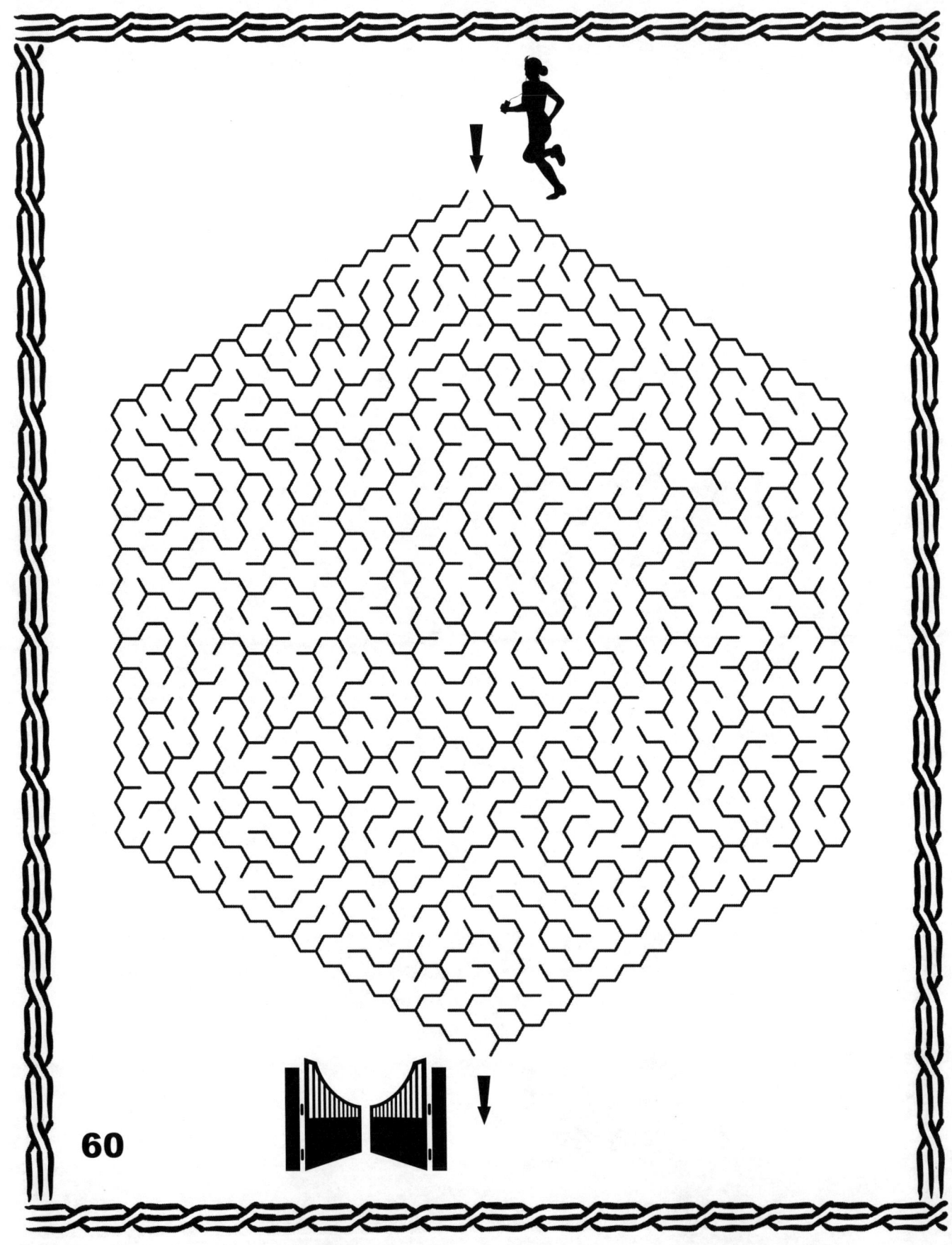

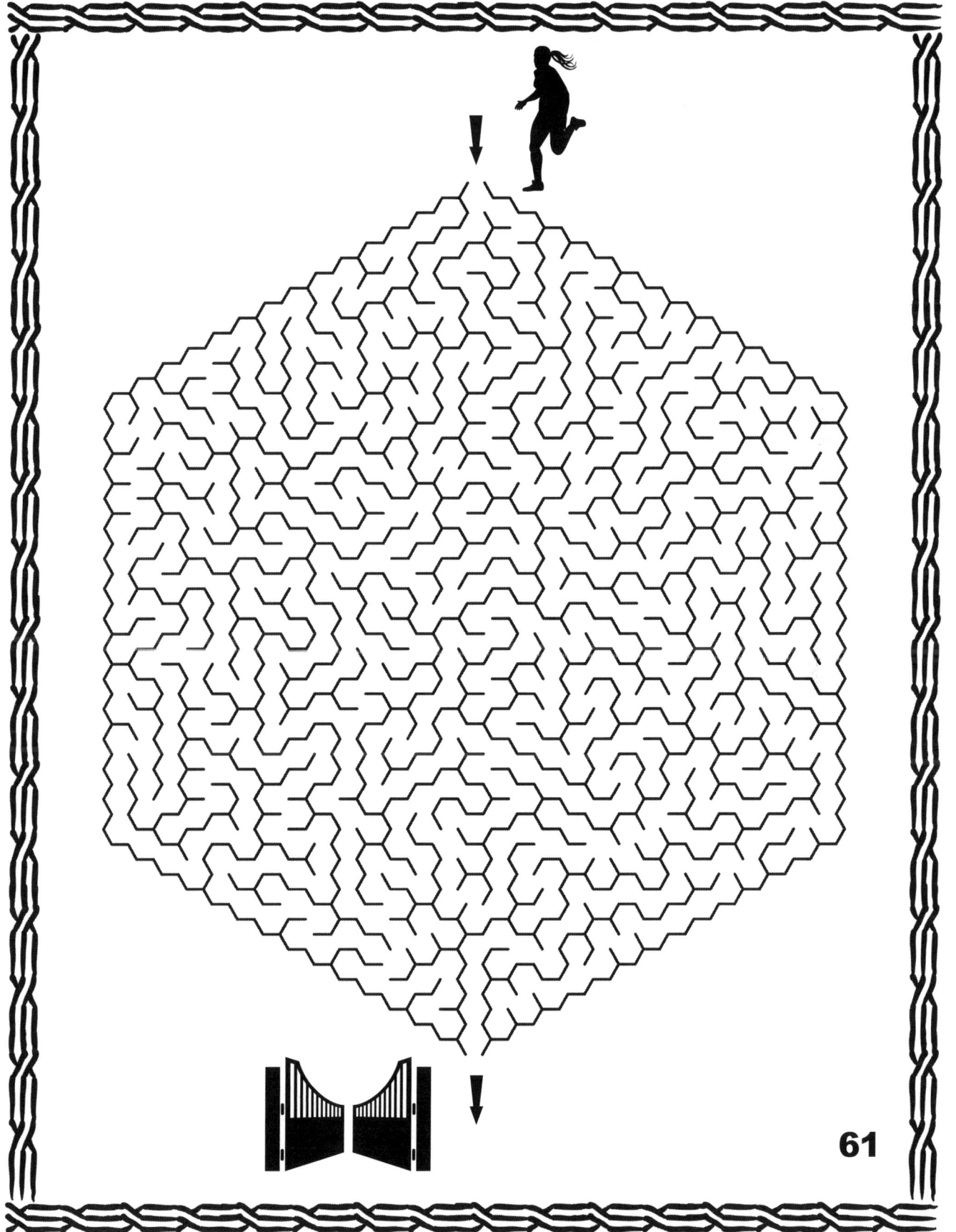

61

62

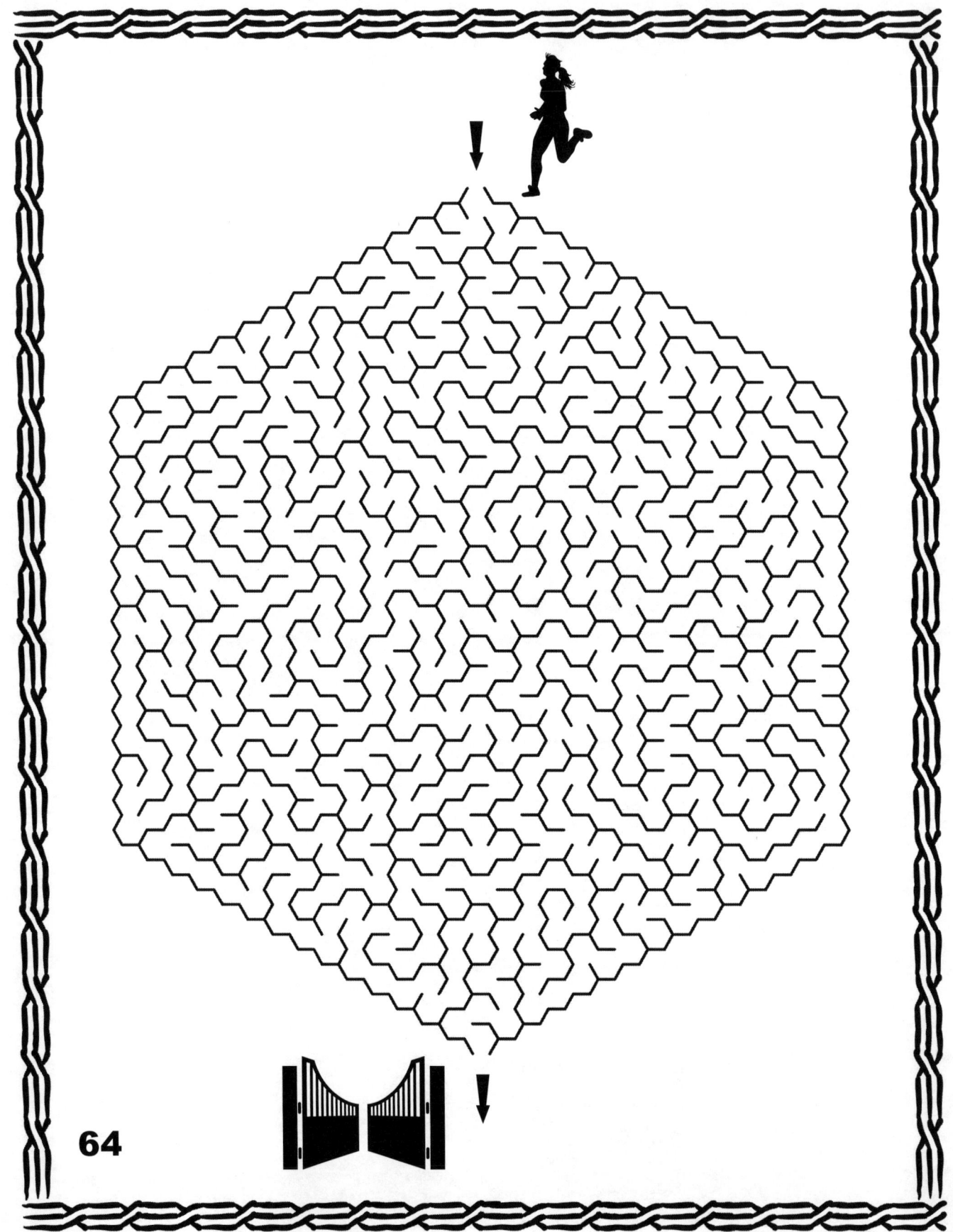

64

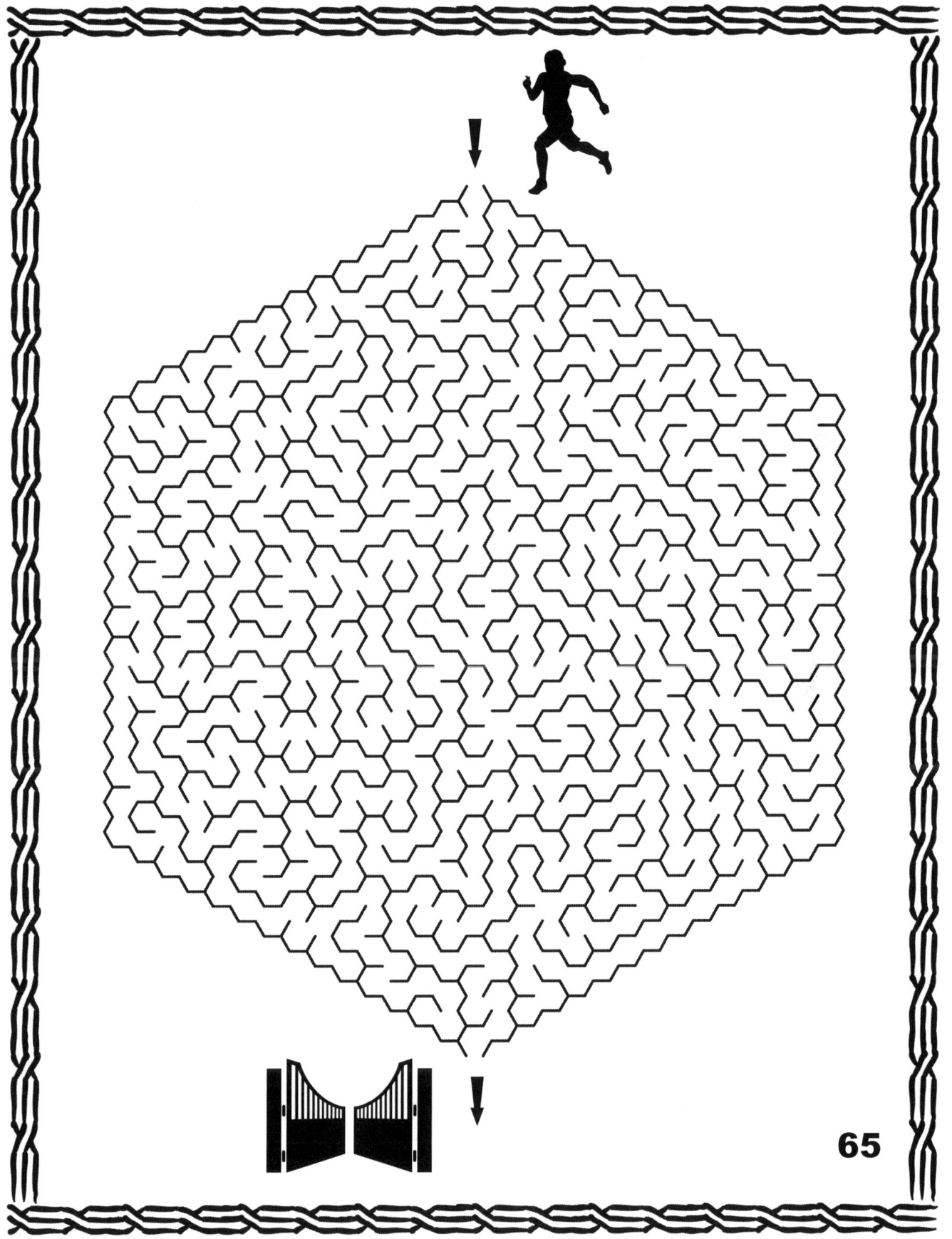

65

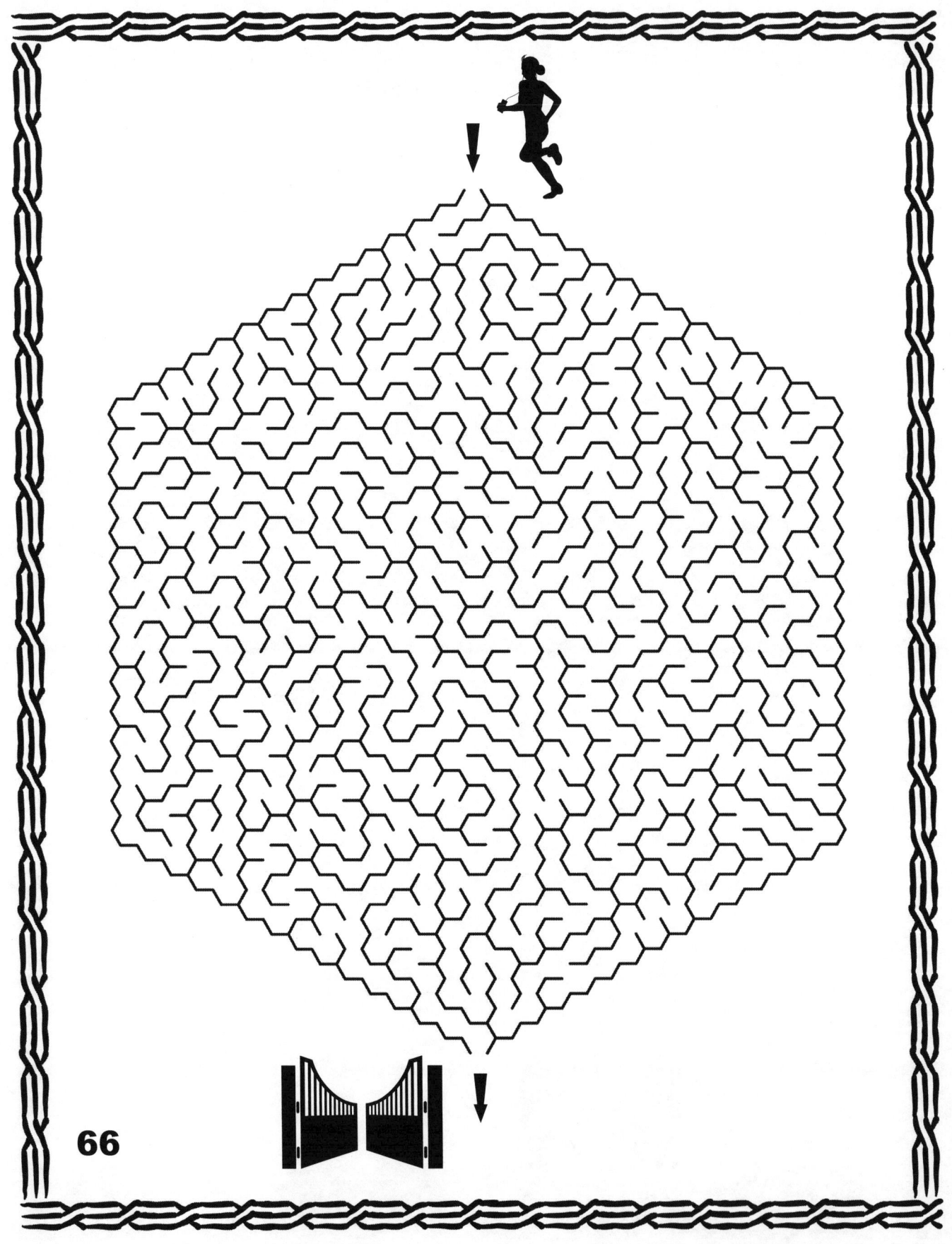

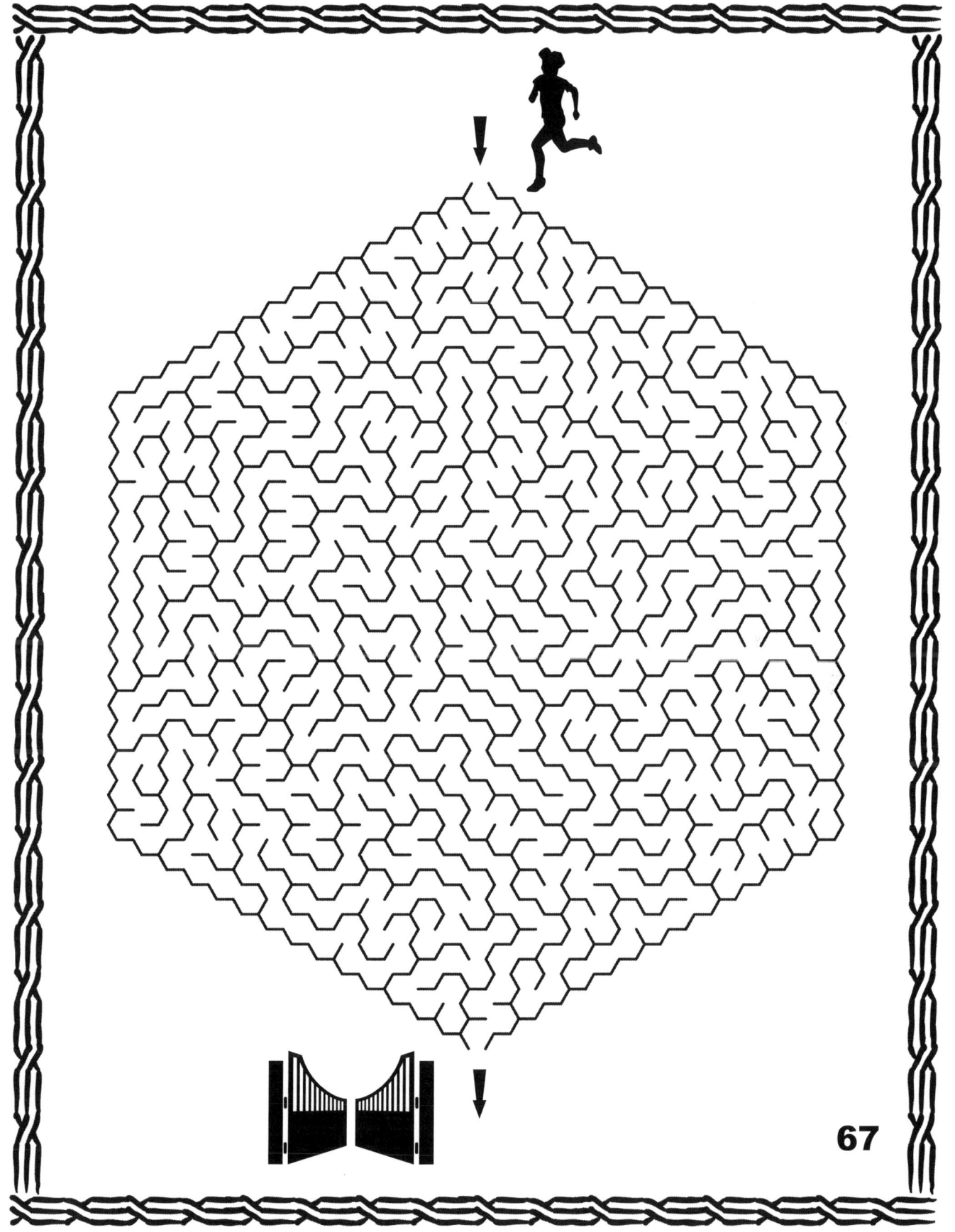

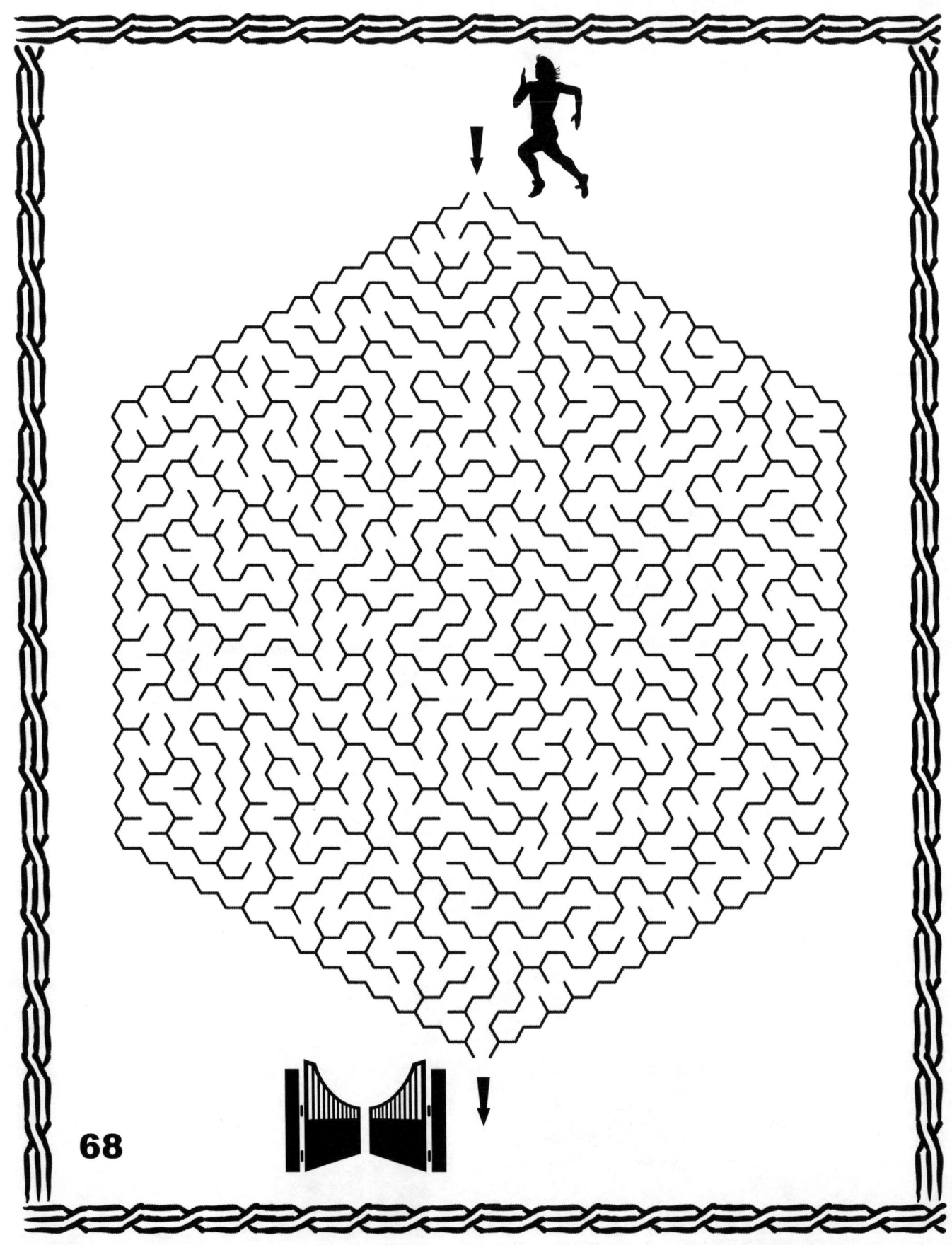

68

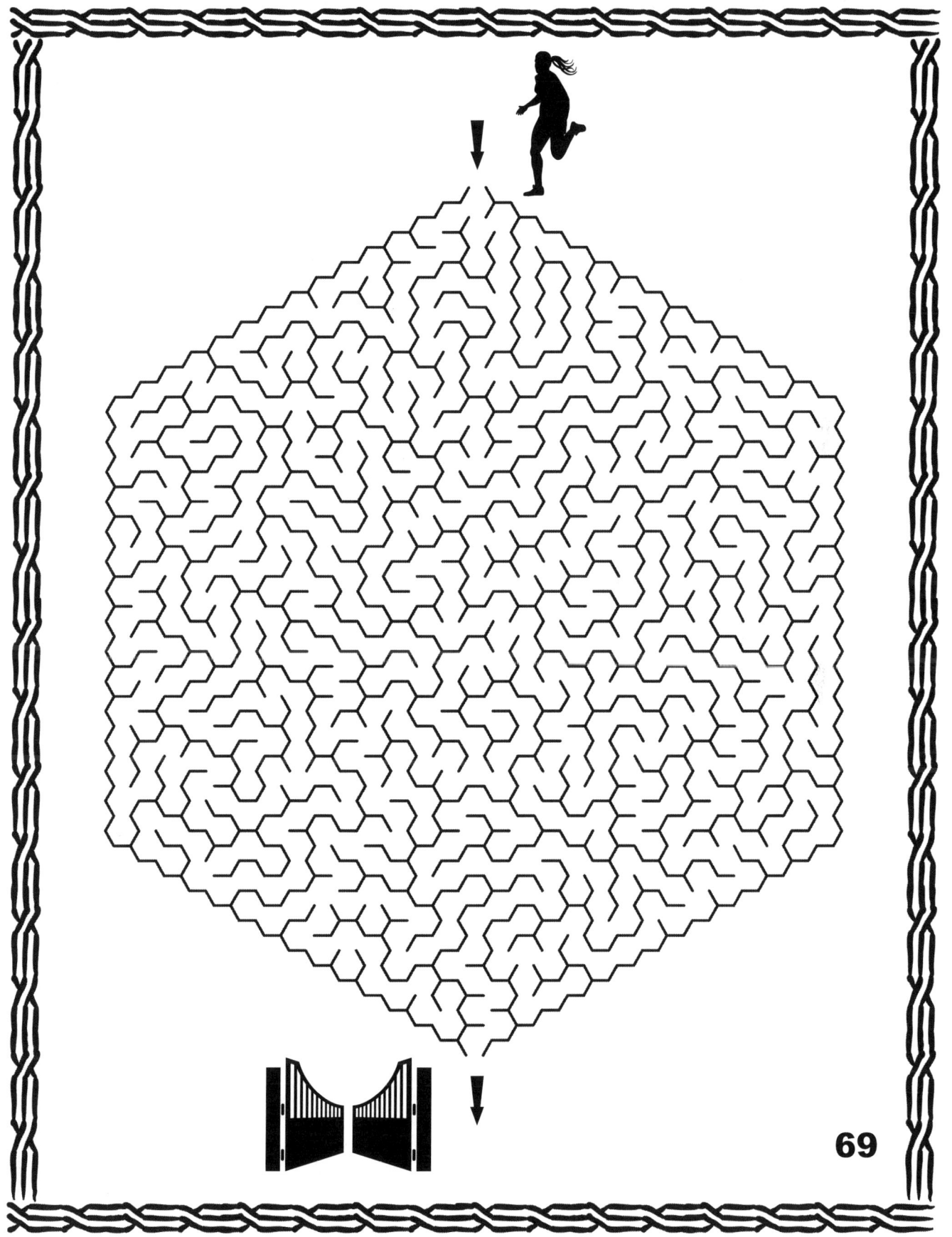

69

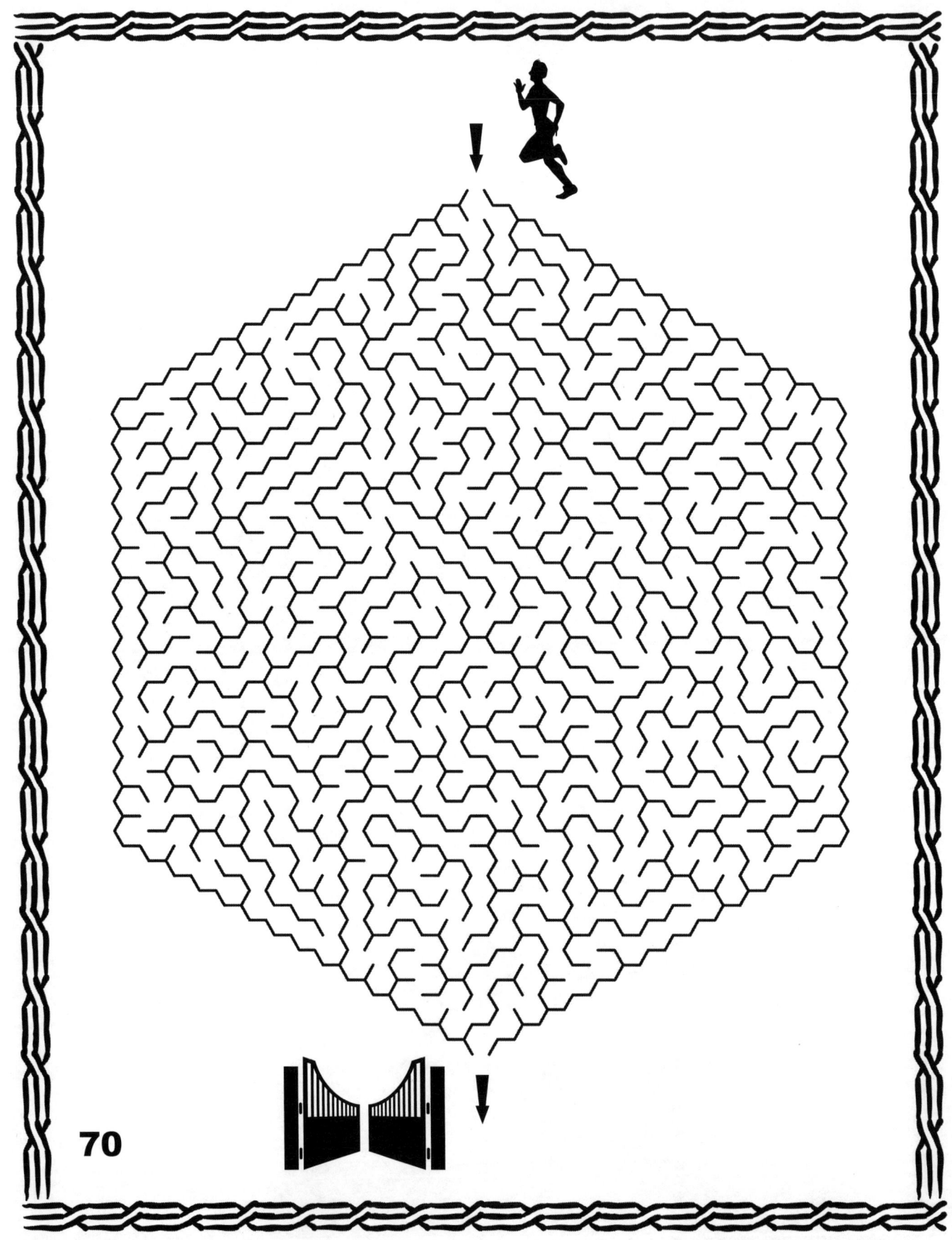

70

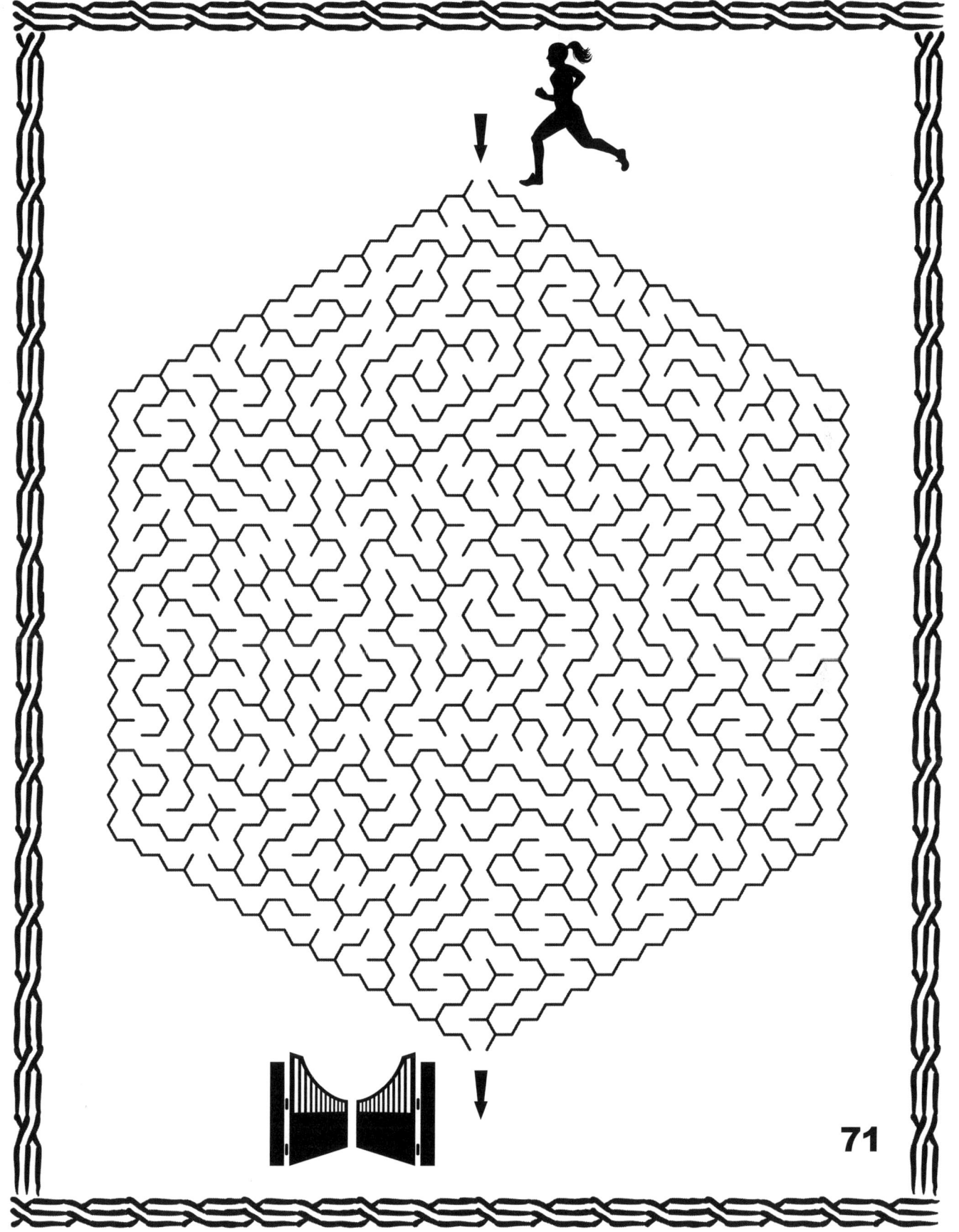

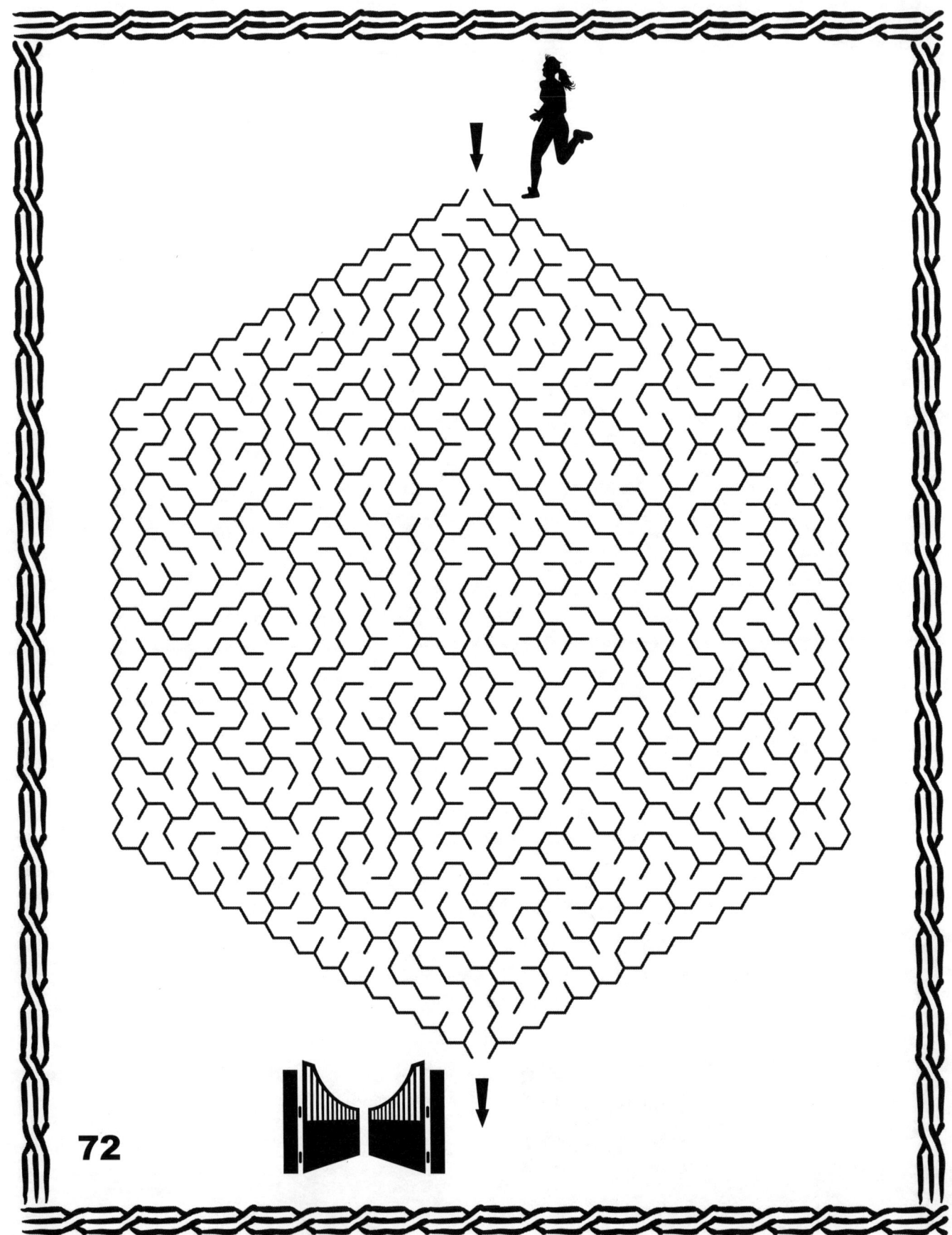

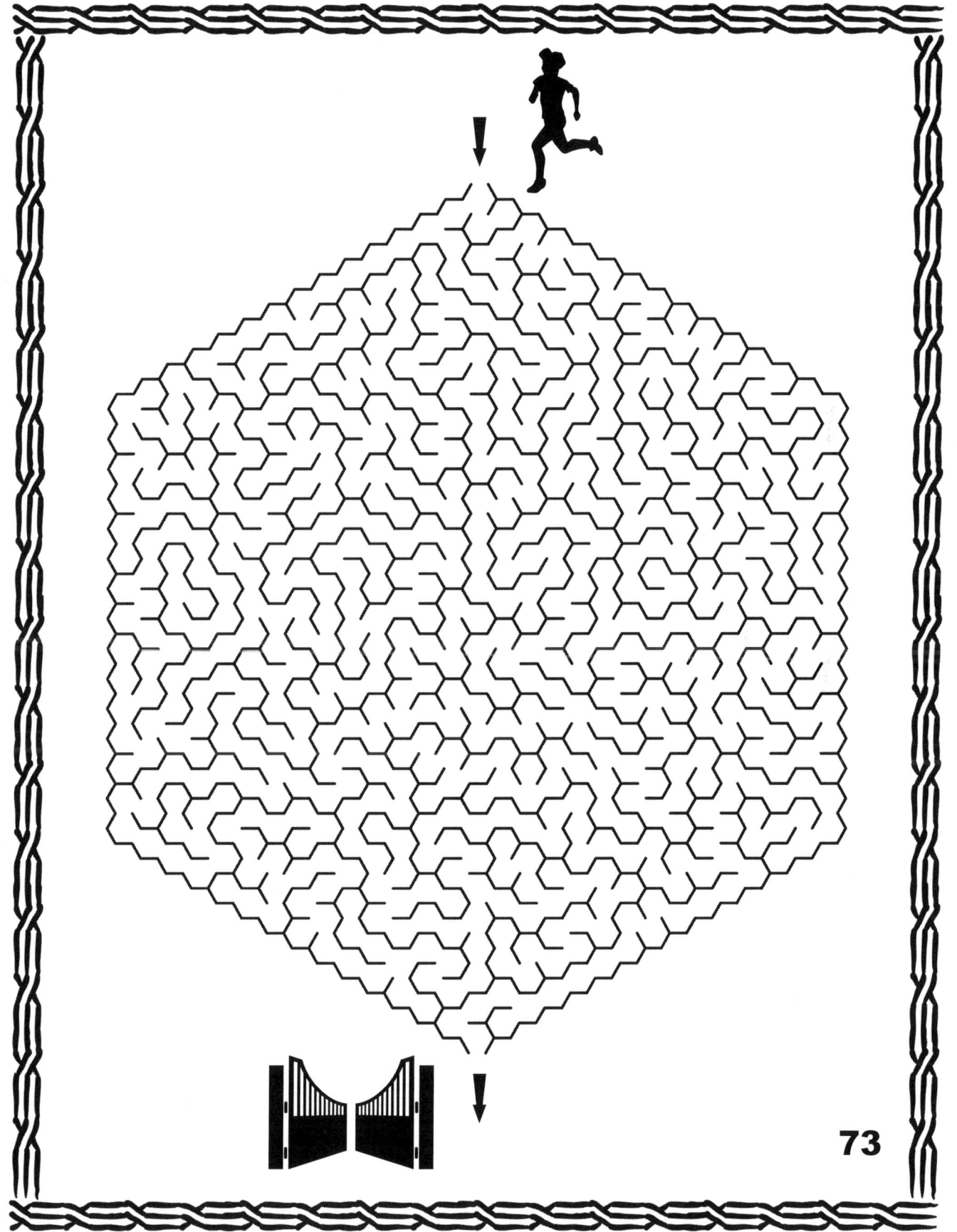

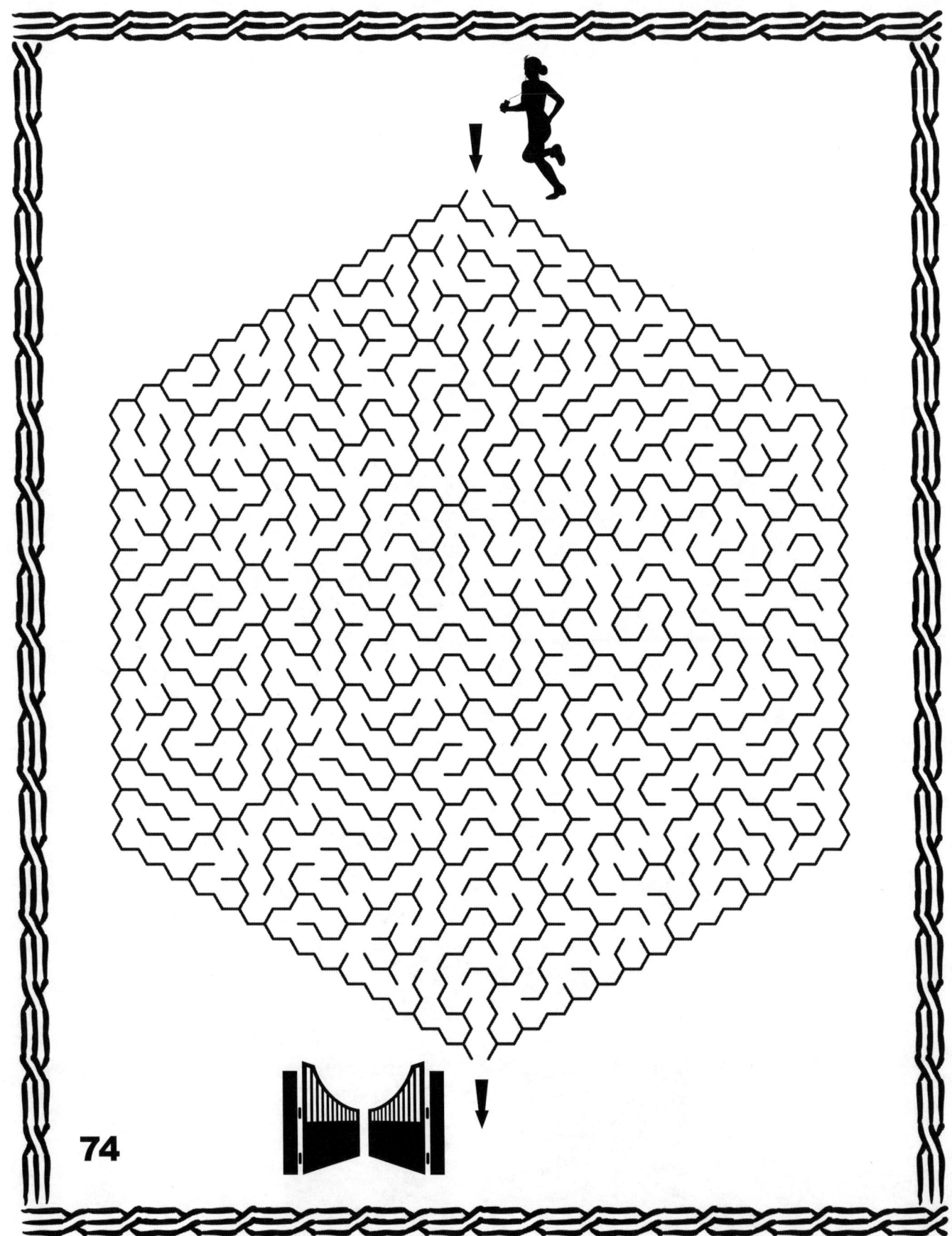

74

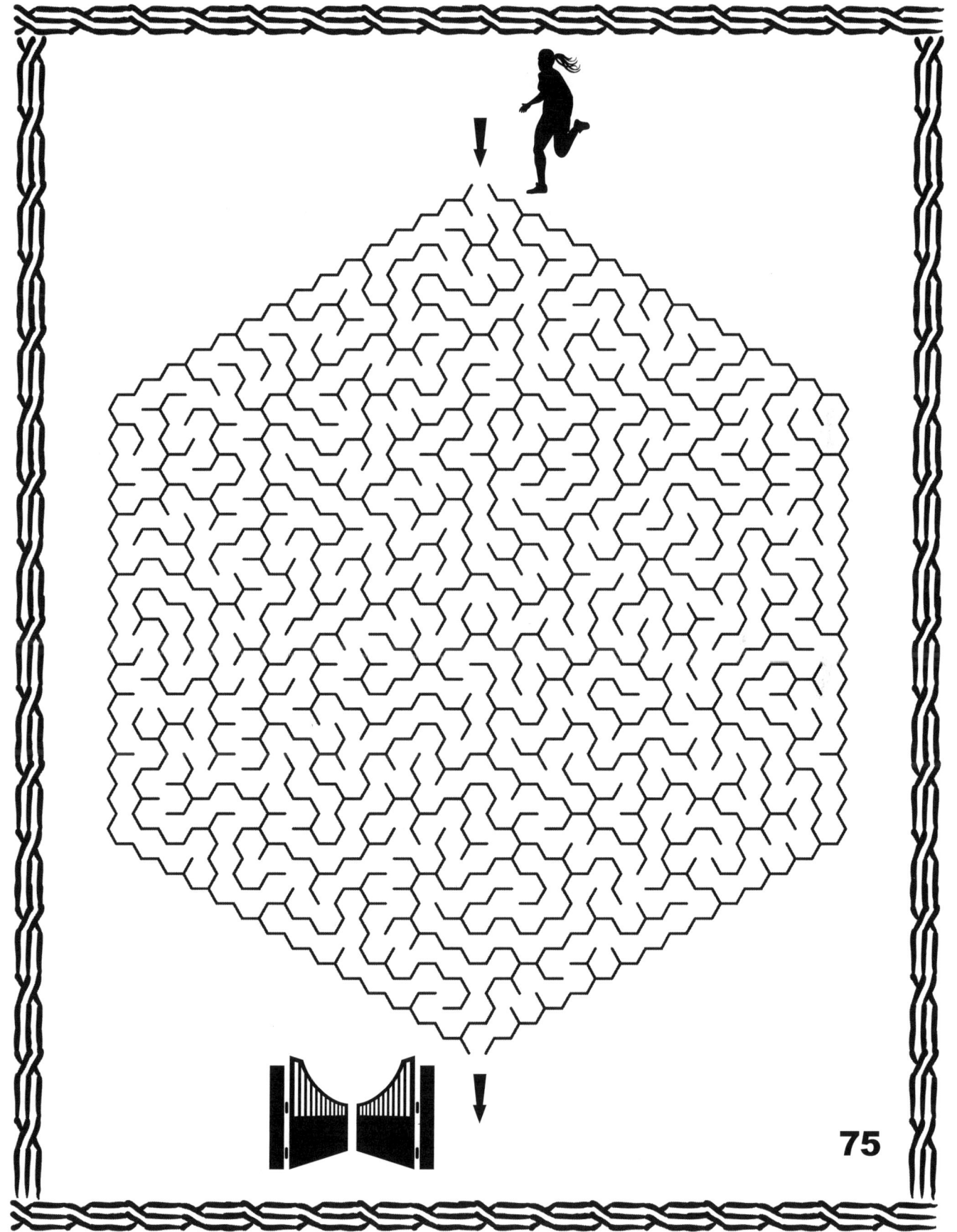

75

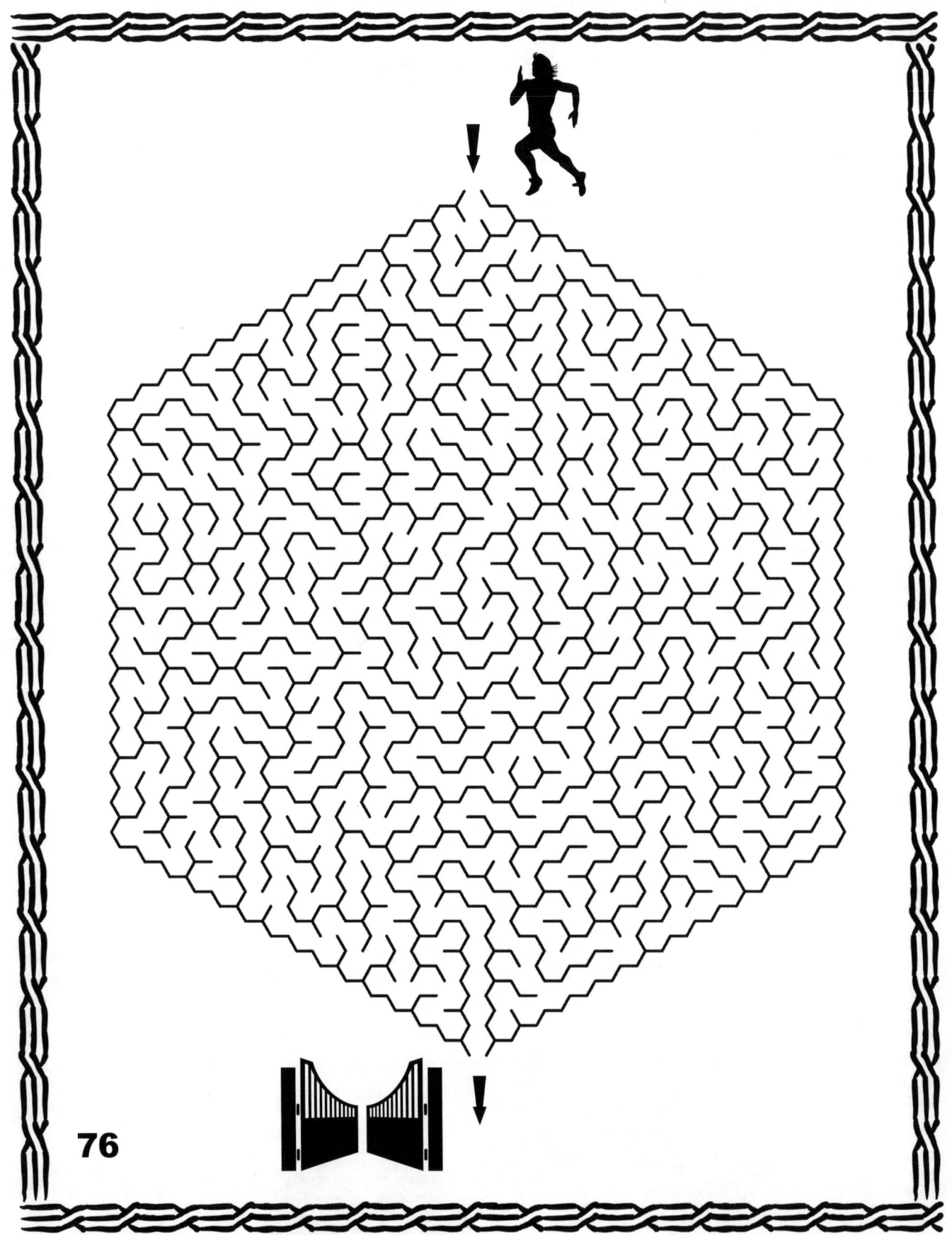

76

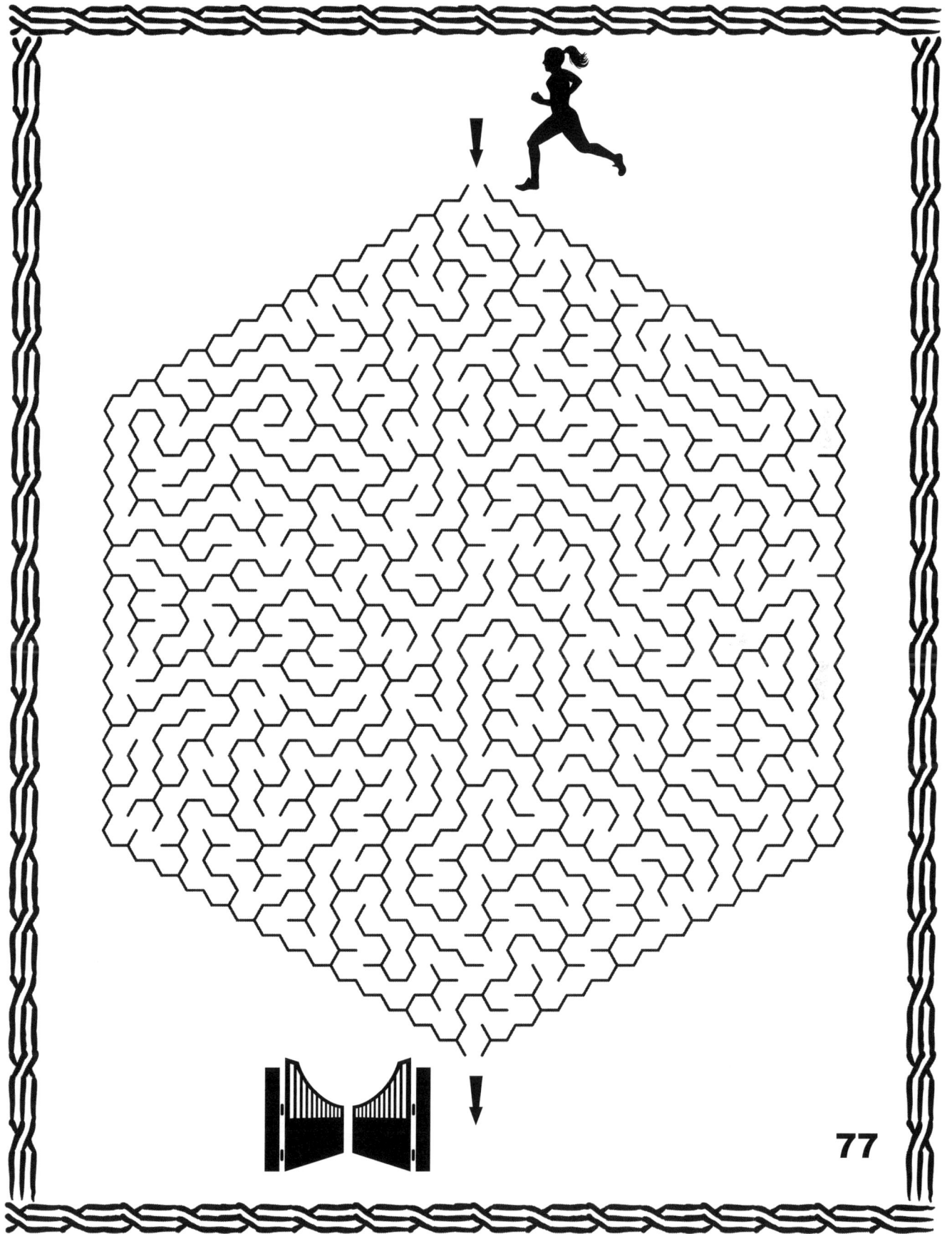

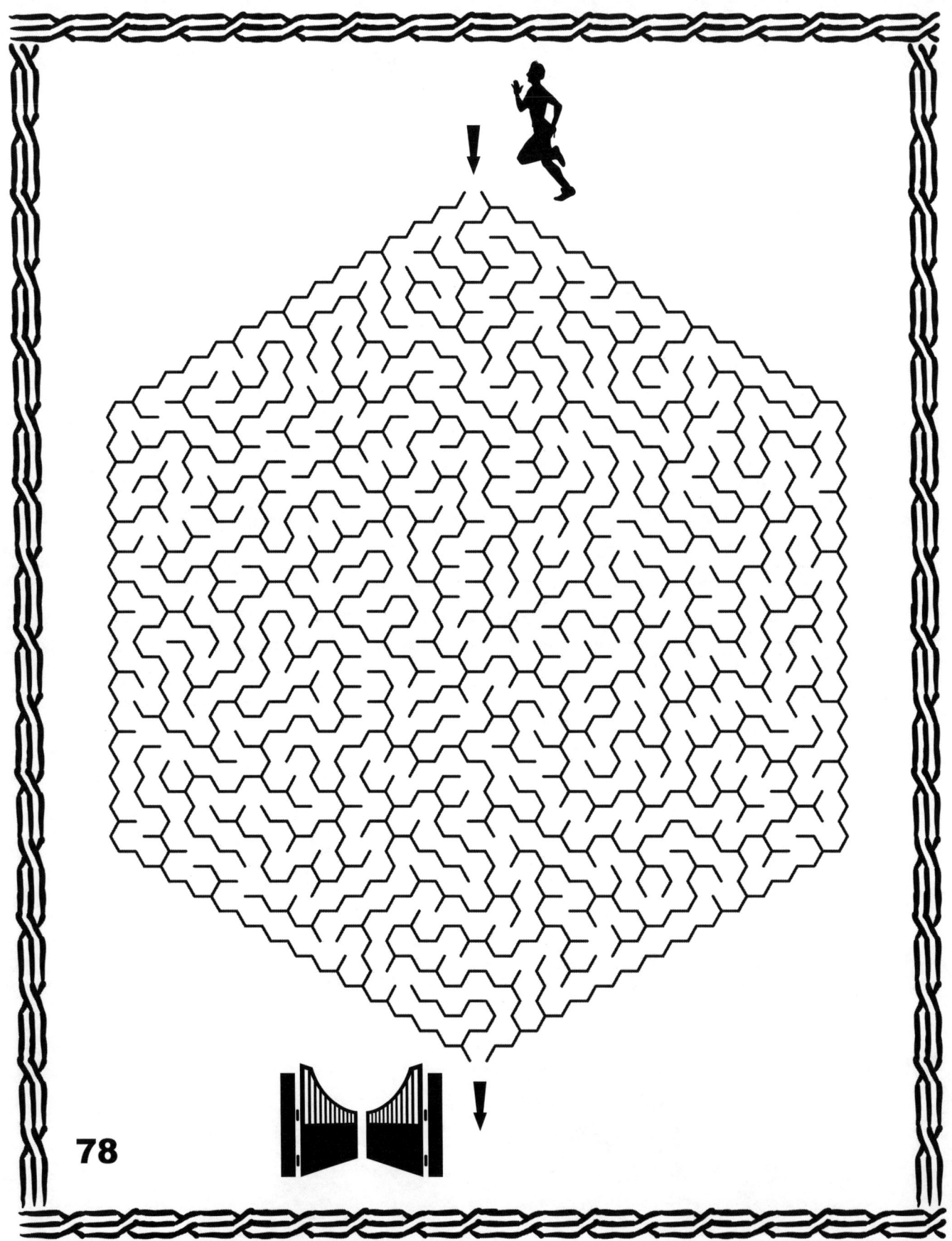

78

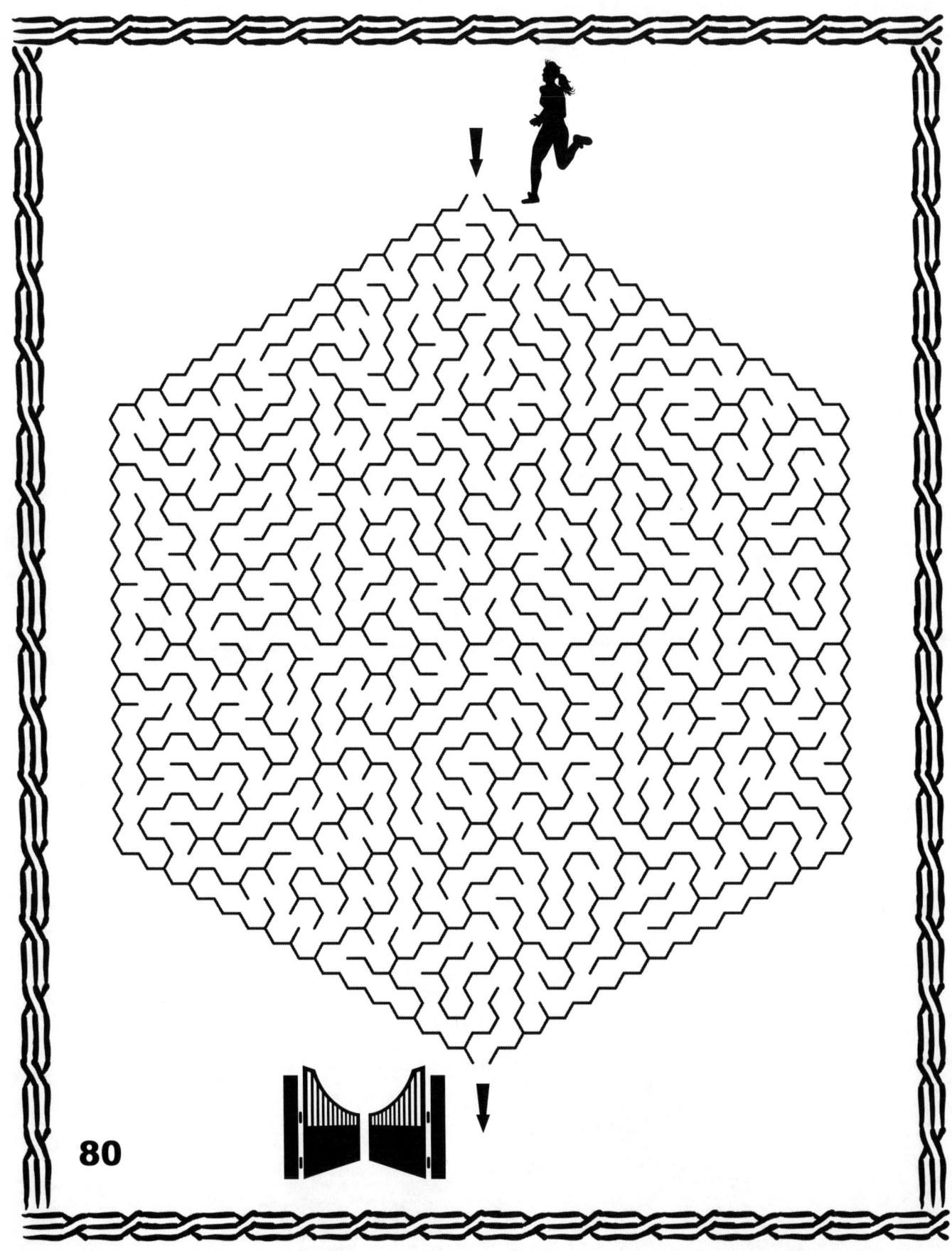

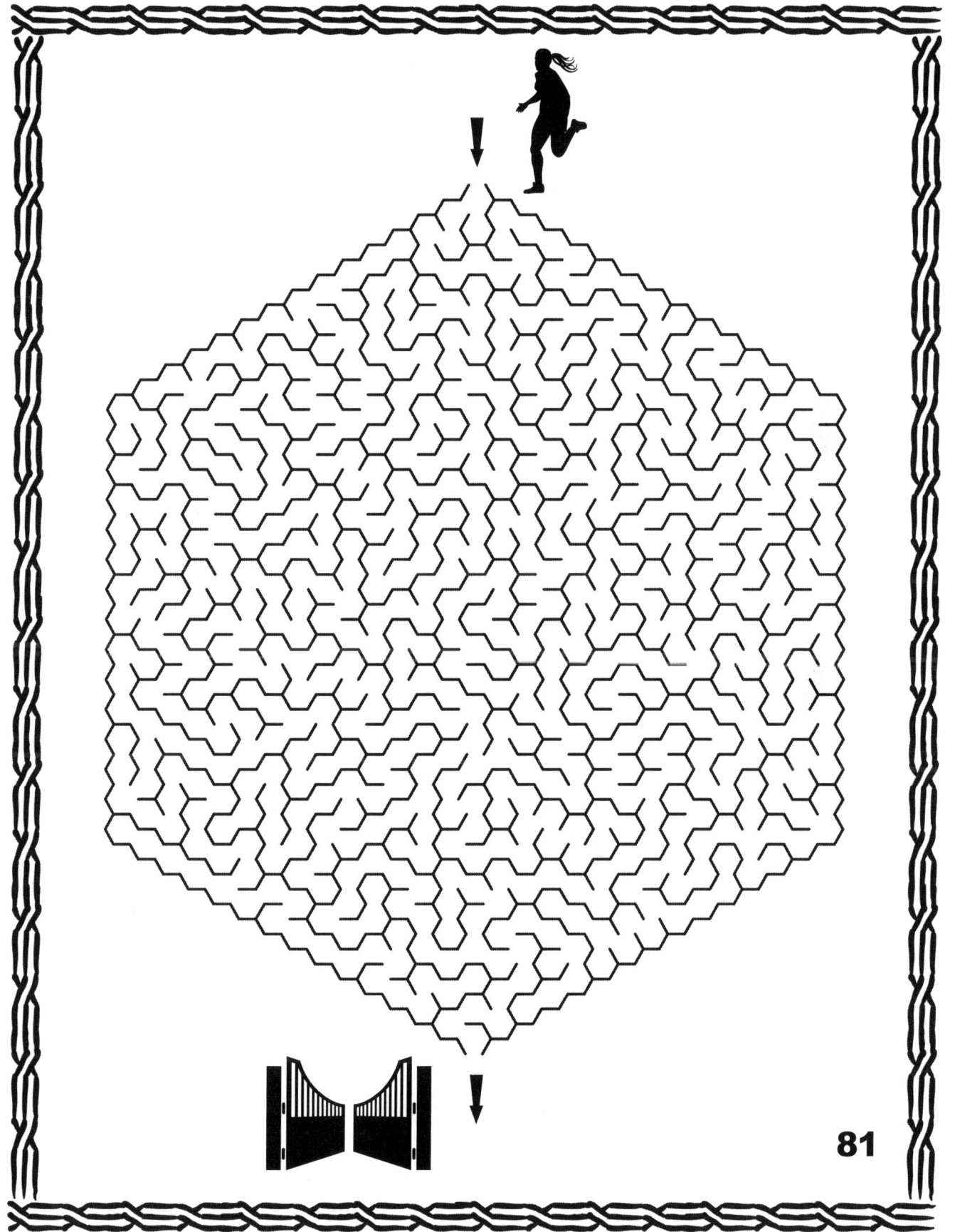

81

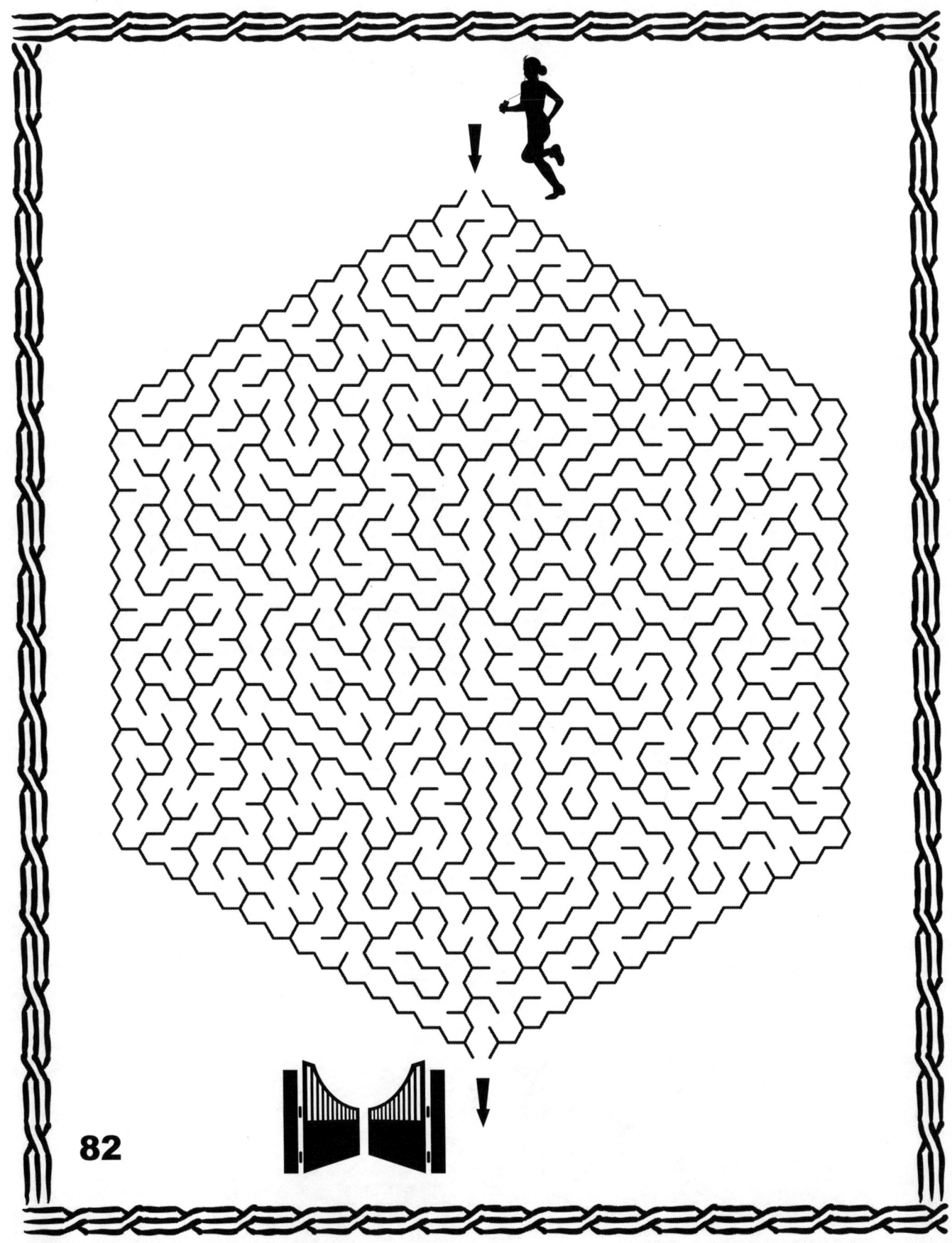

82

1

2

3

4

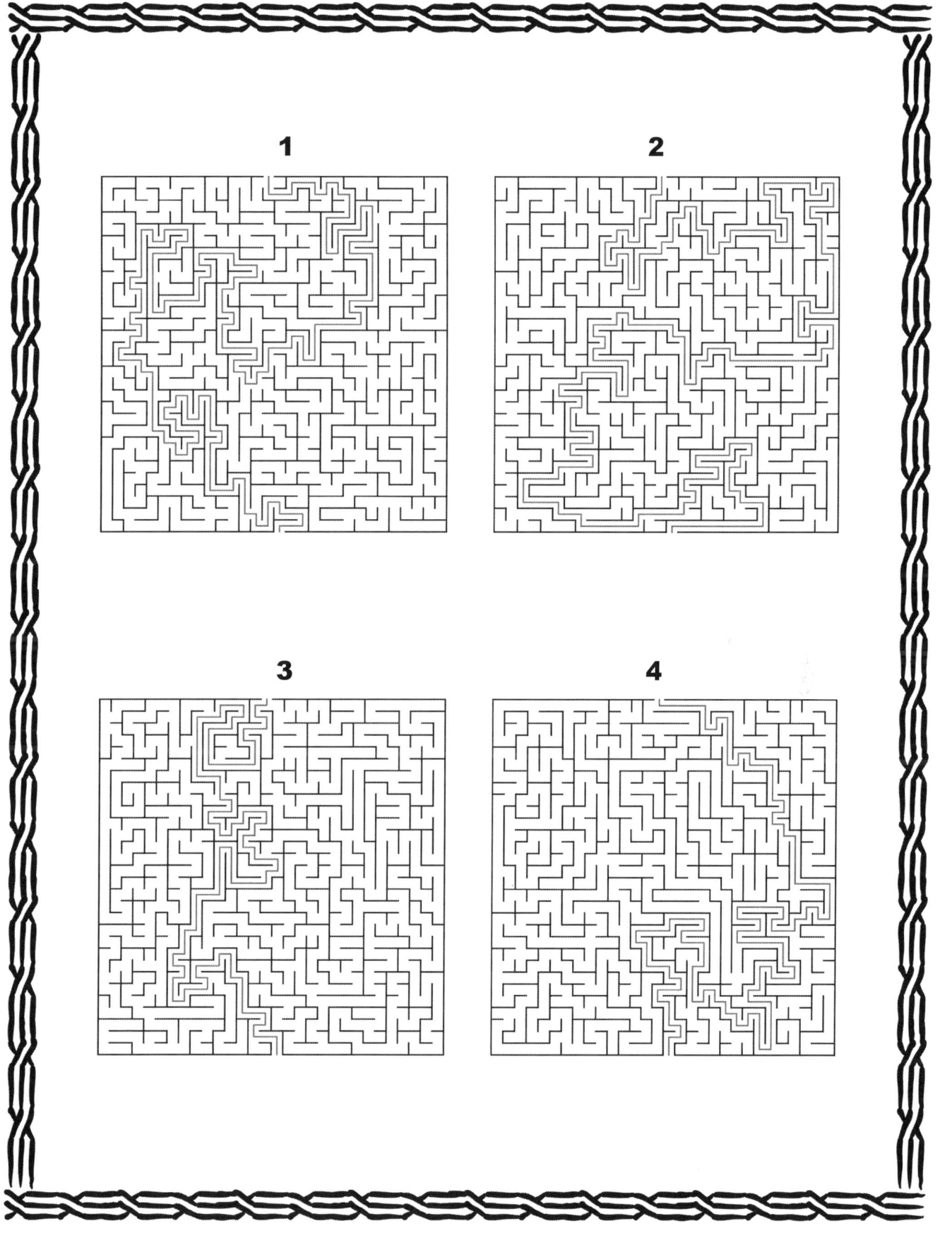

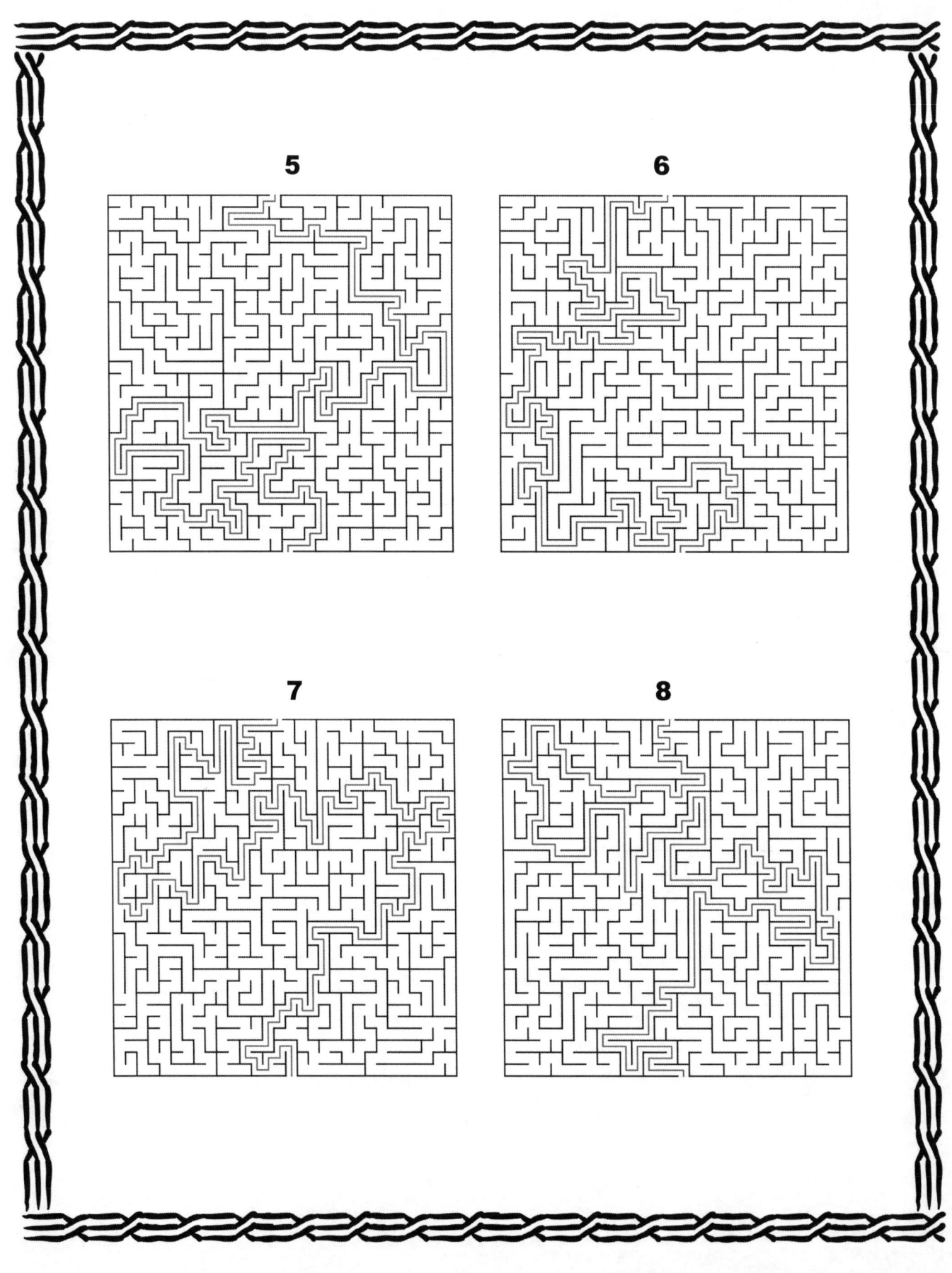

5

6

7

8

9

10

11

12

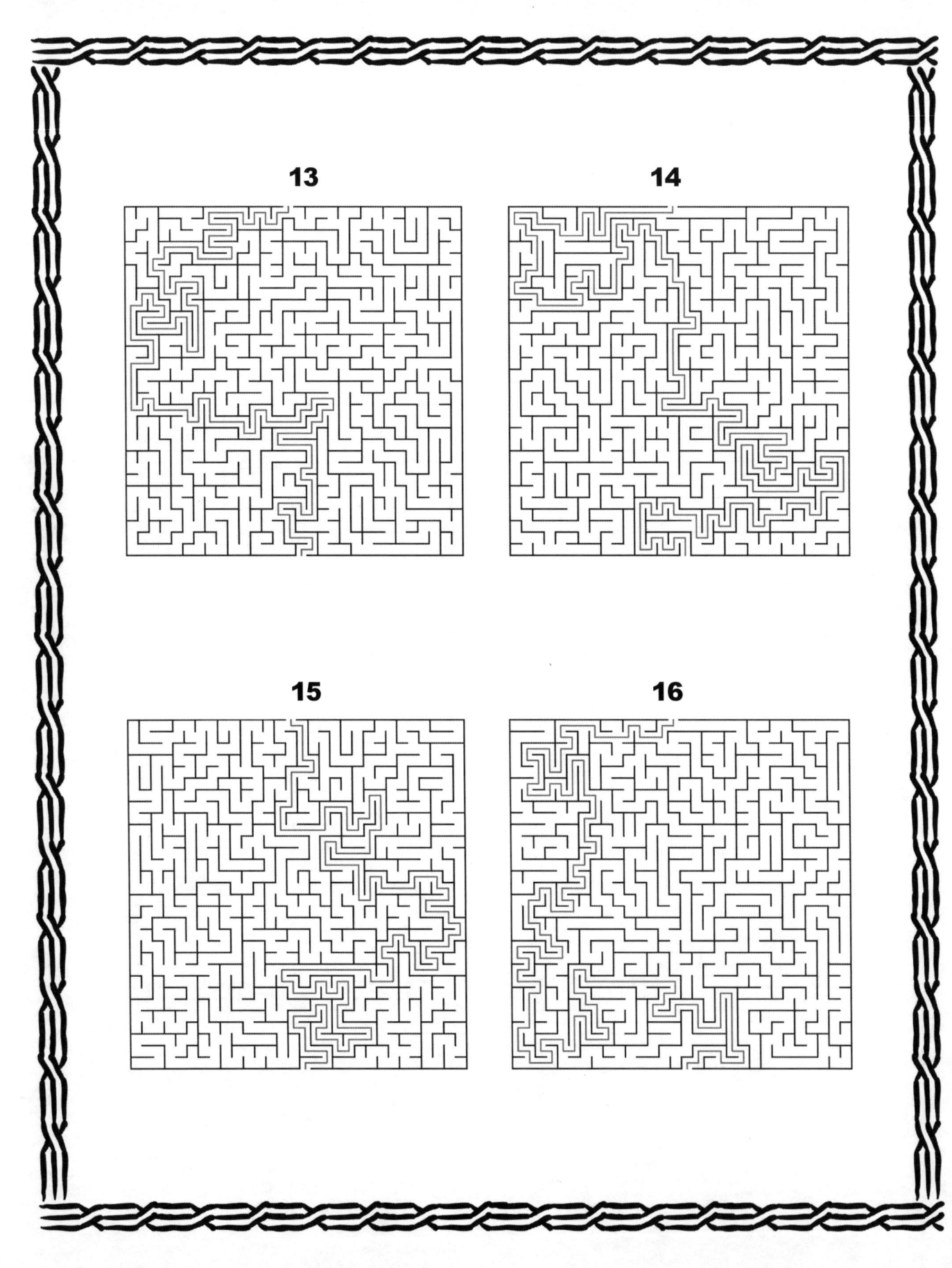

13

14

15

16

17

18

19

20

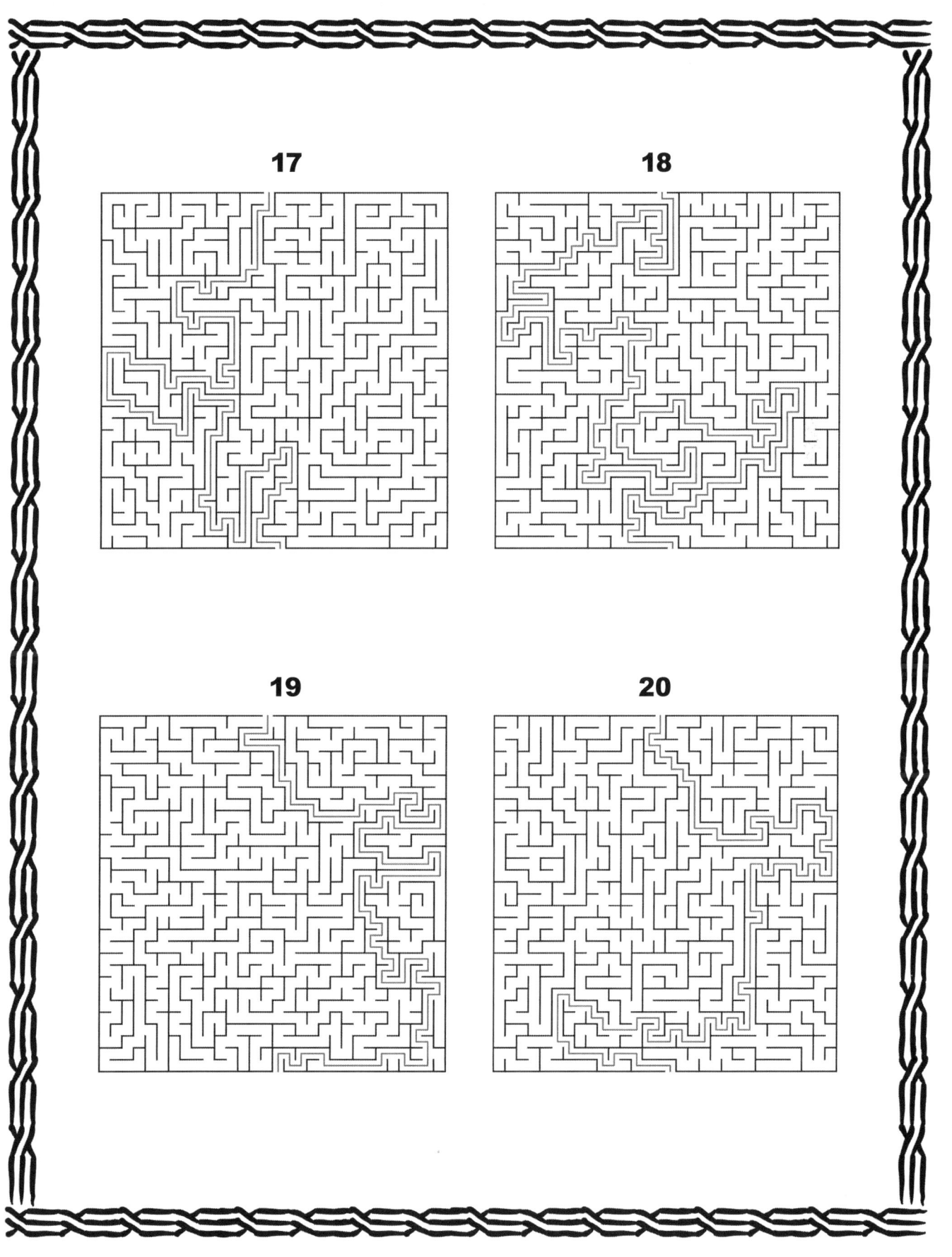

21

22

23

24

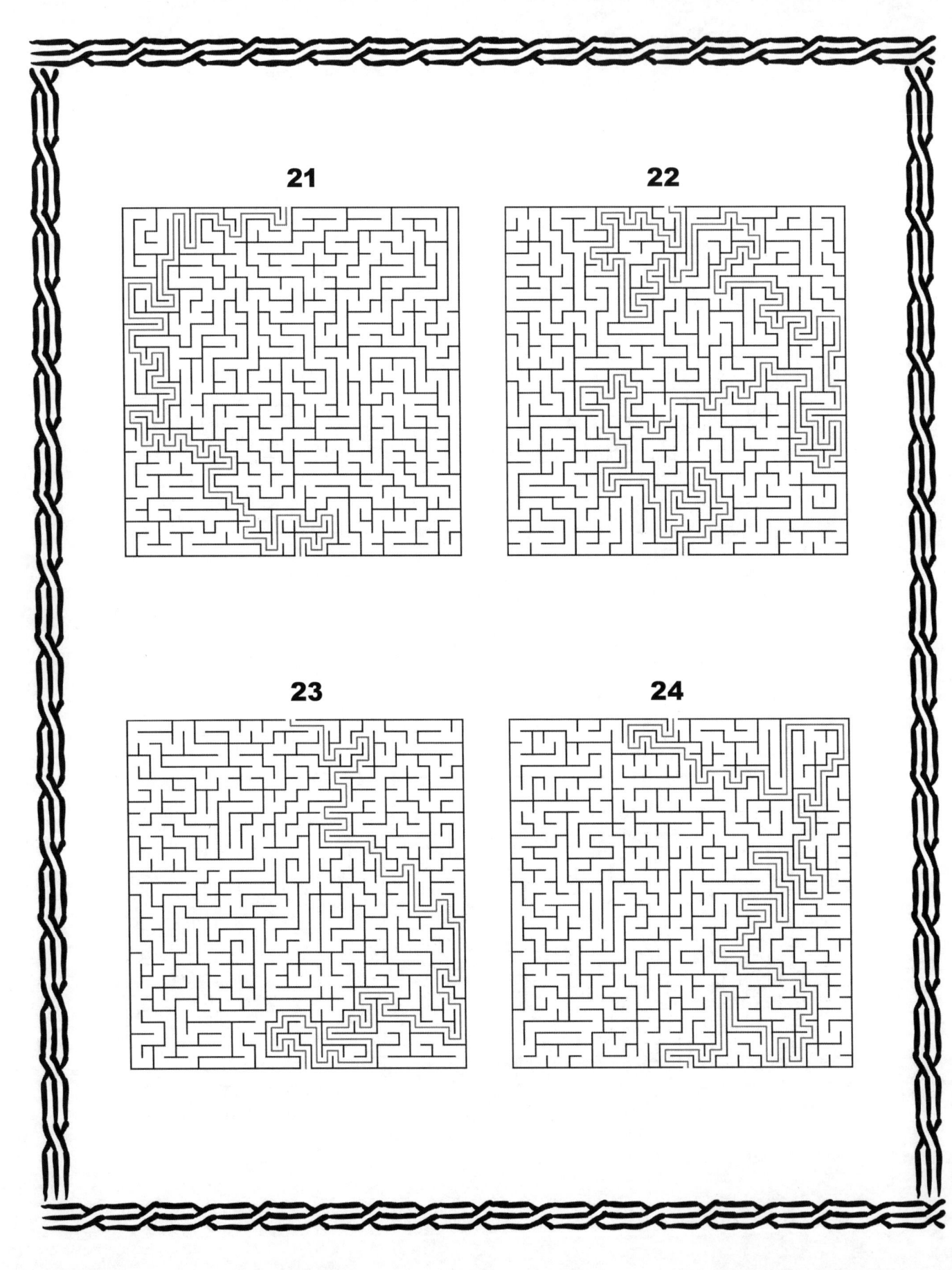

25

26

27

28

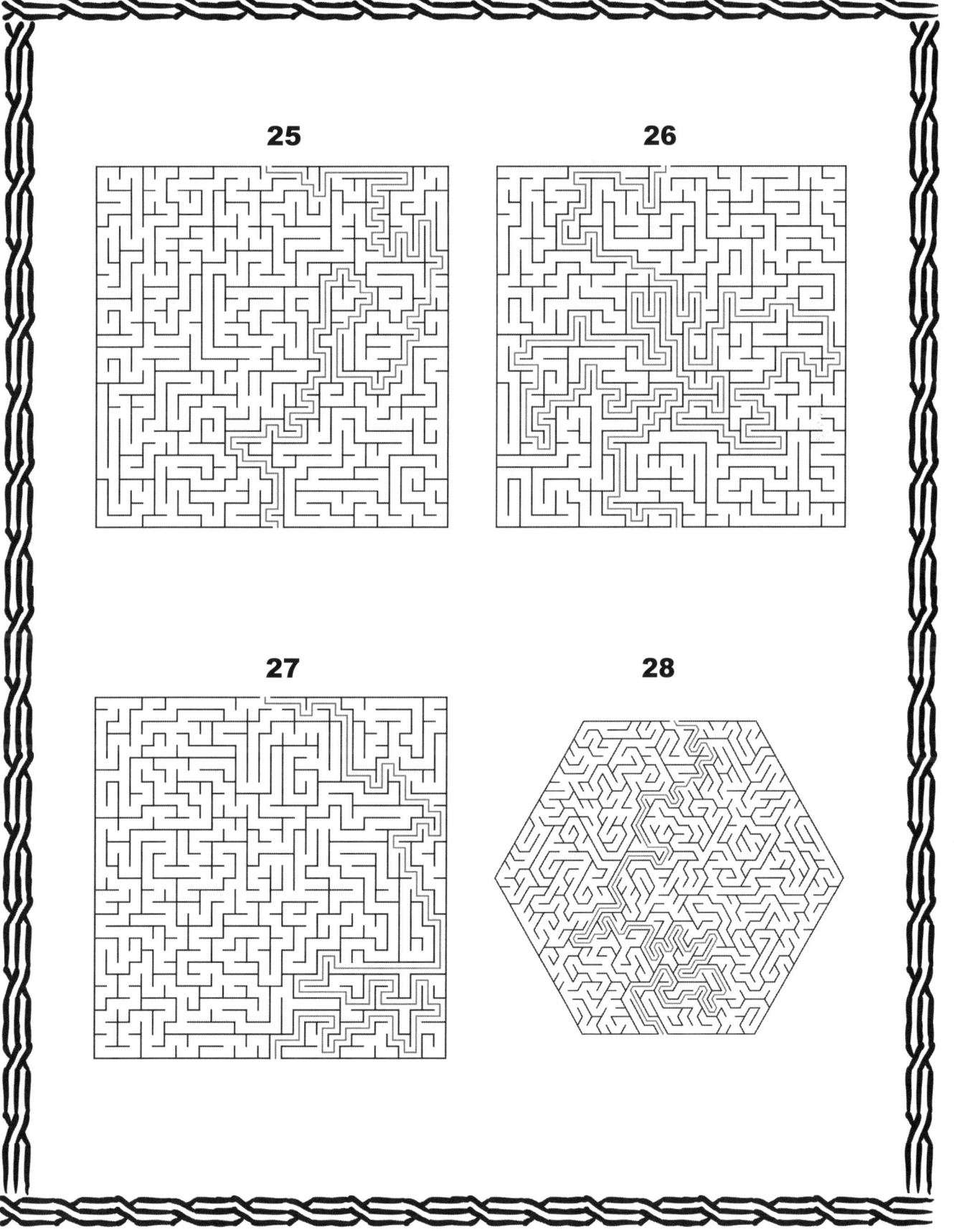

29

30

31

32

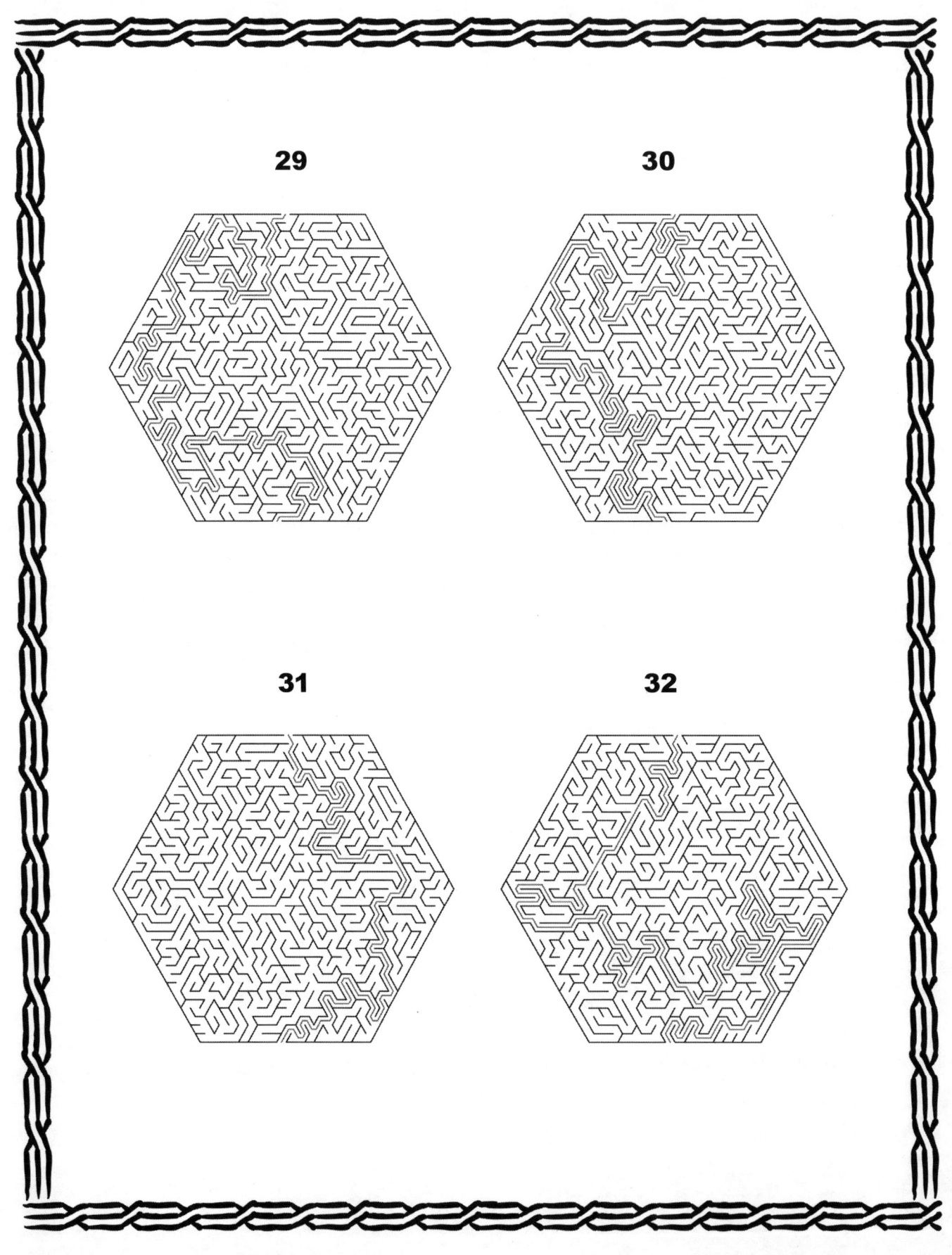

33

34

35

36

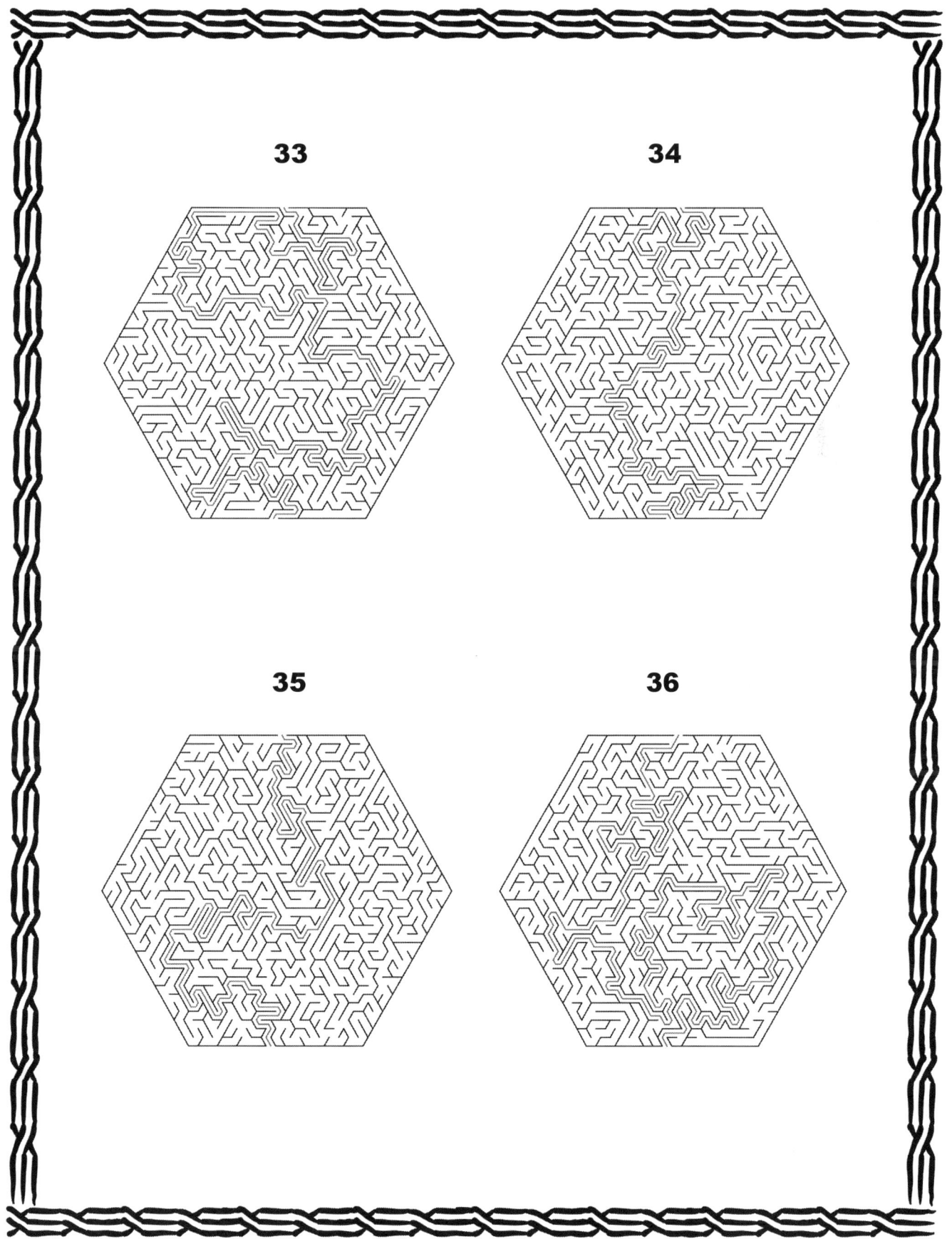

37

38

39

40

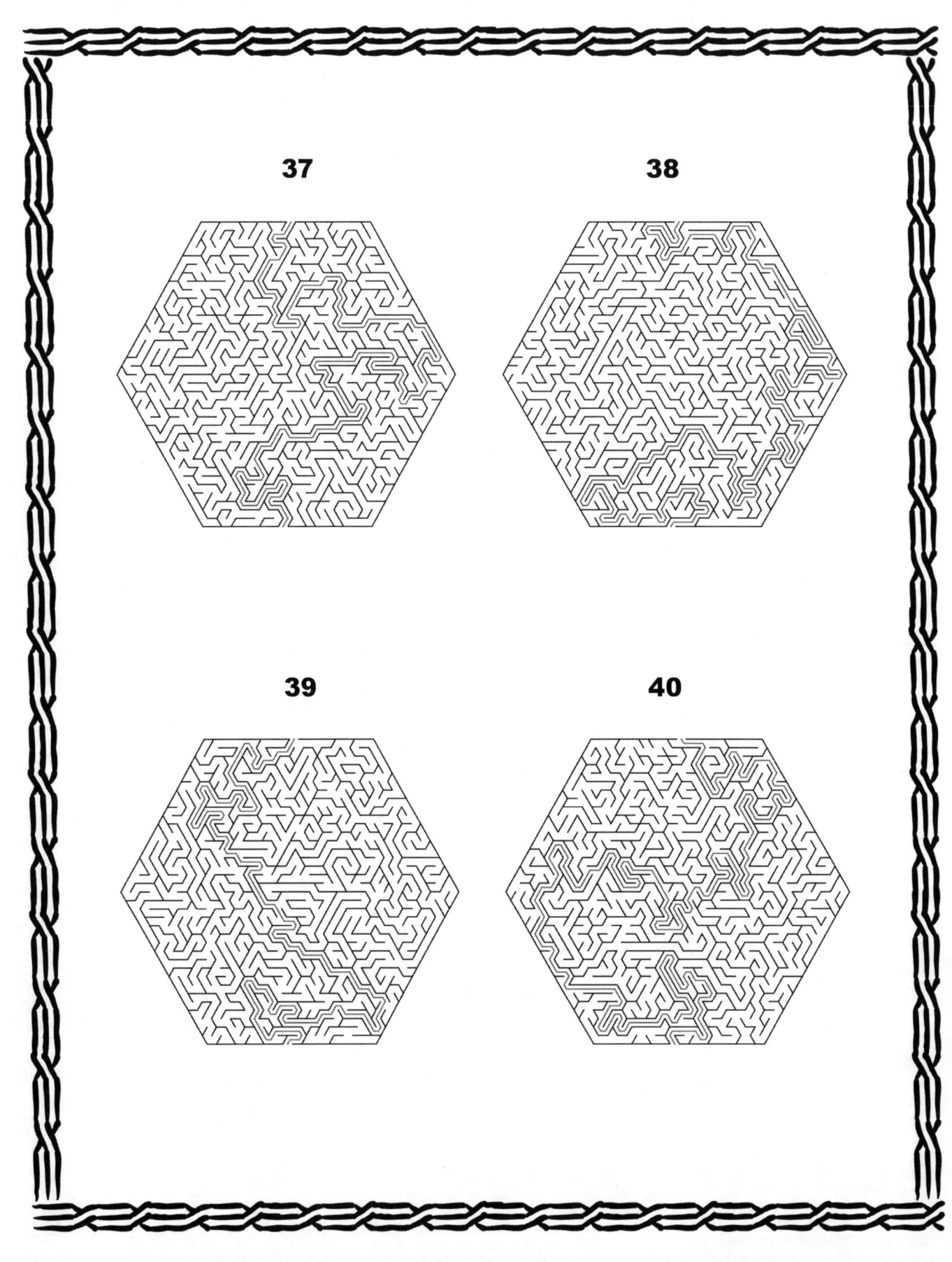

41

42

43

44

45

46

47

48

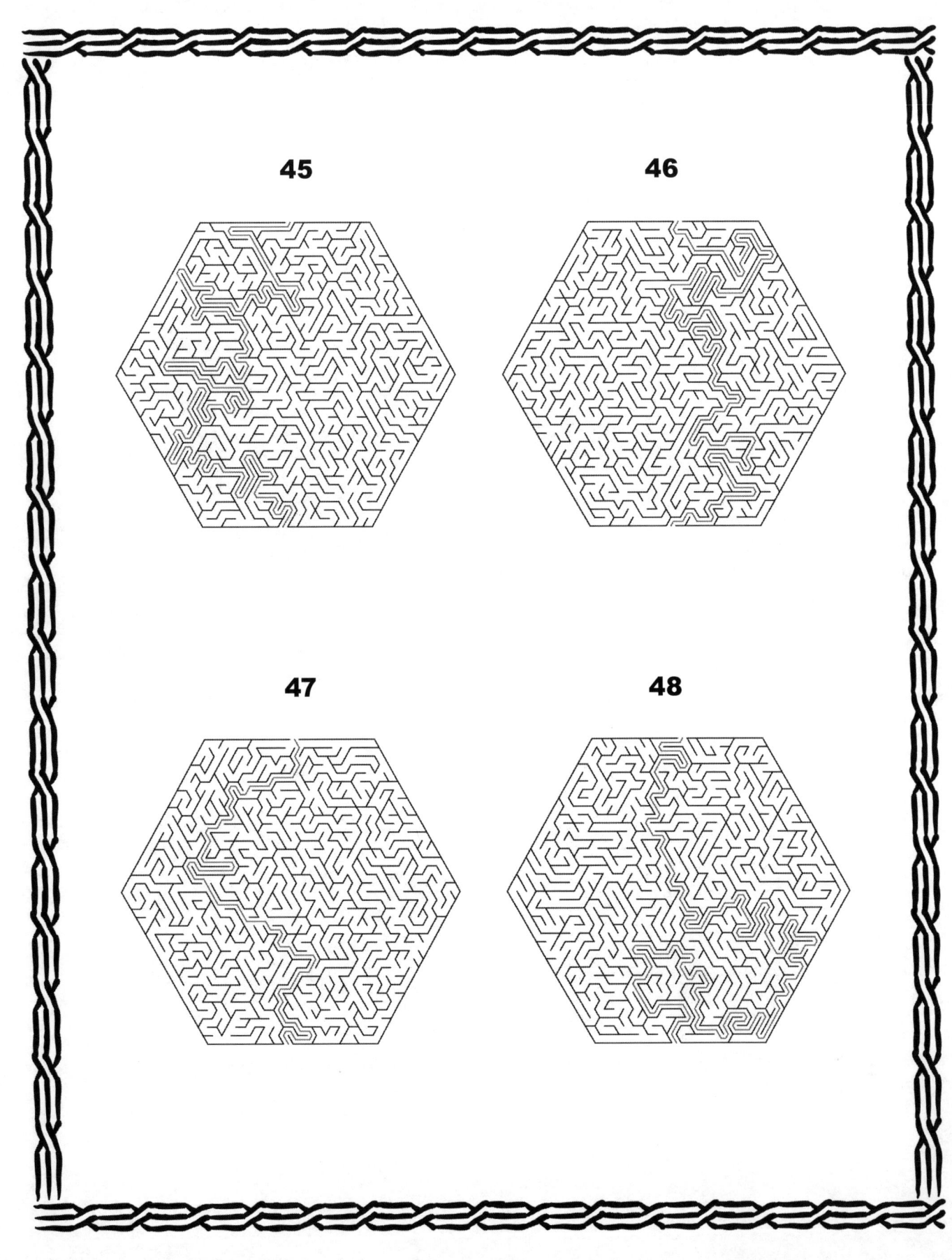

49

50

51

52

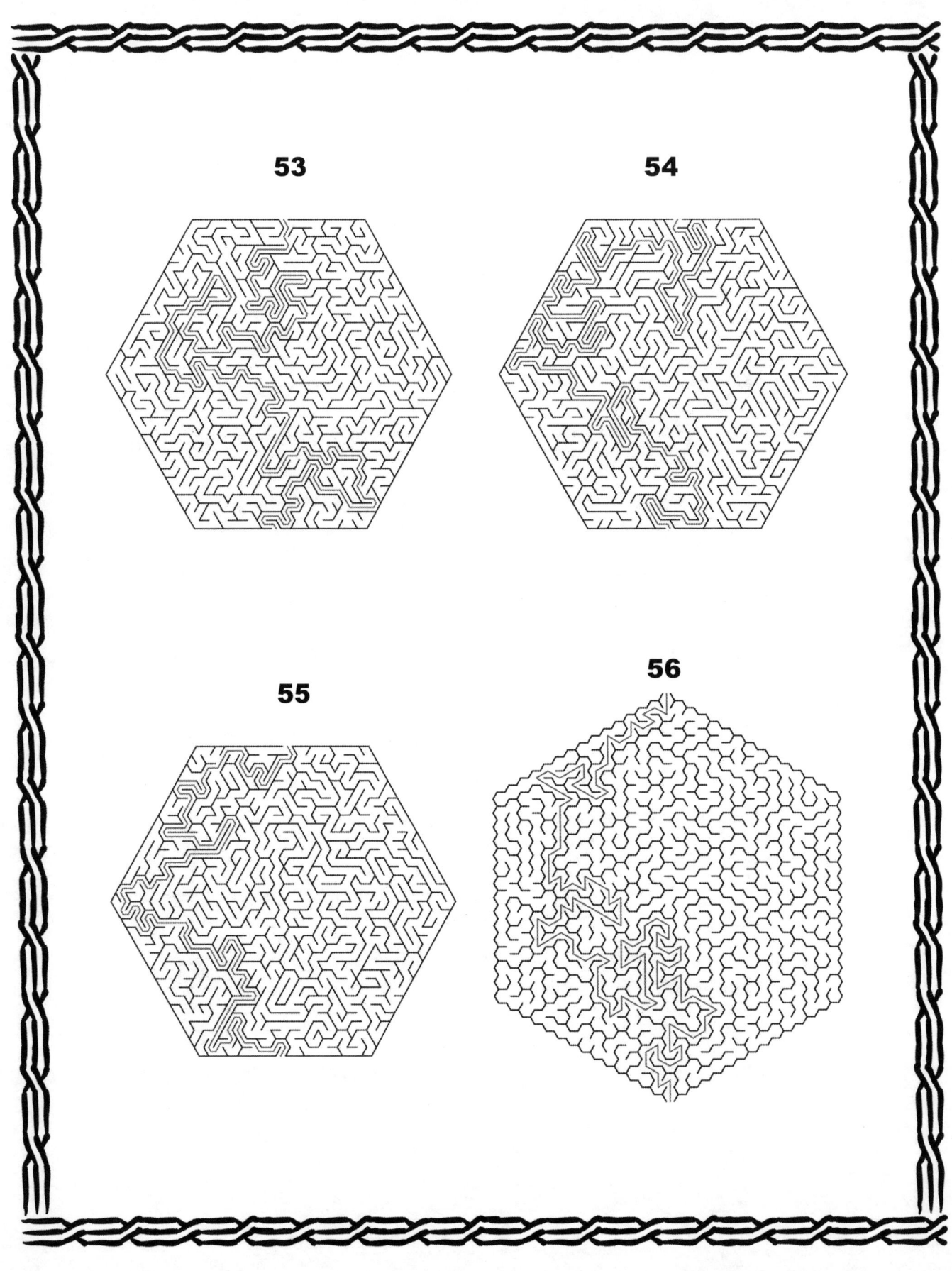

53

54

55

56

57

58

59

60

61 **62**

63 **64**

65

66

67

68

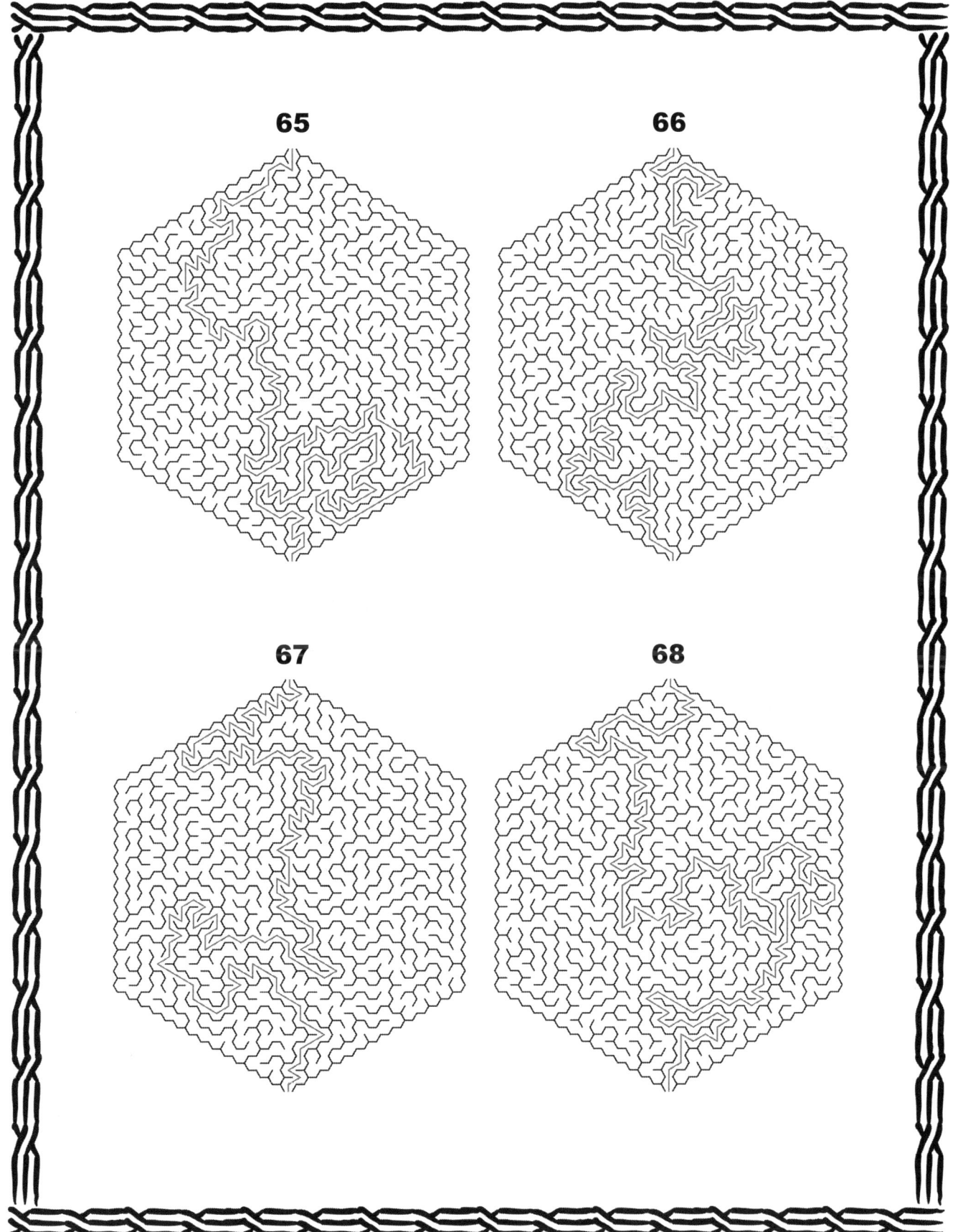

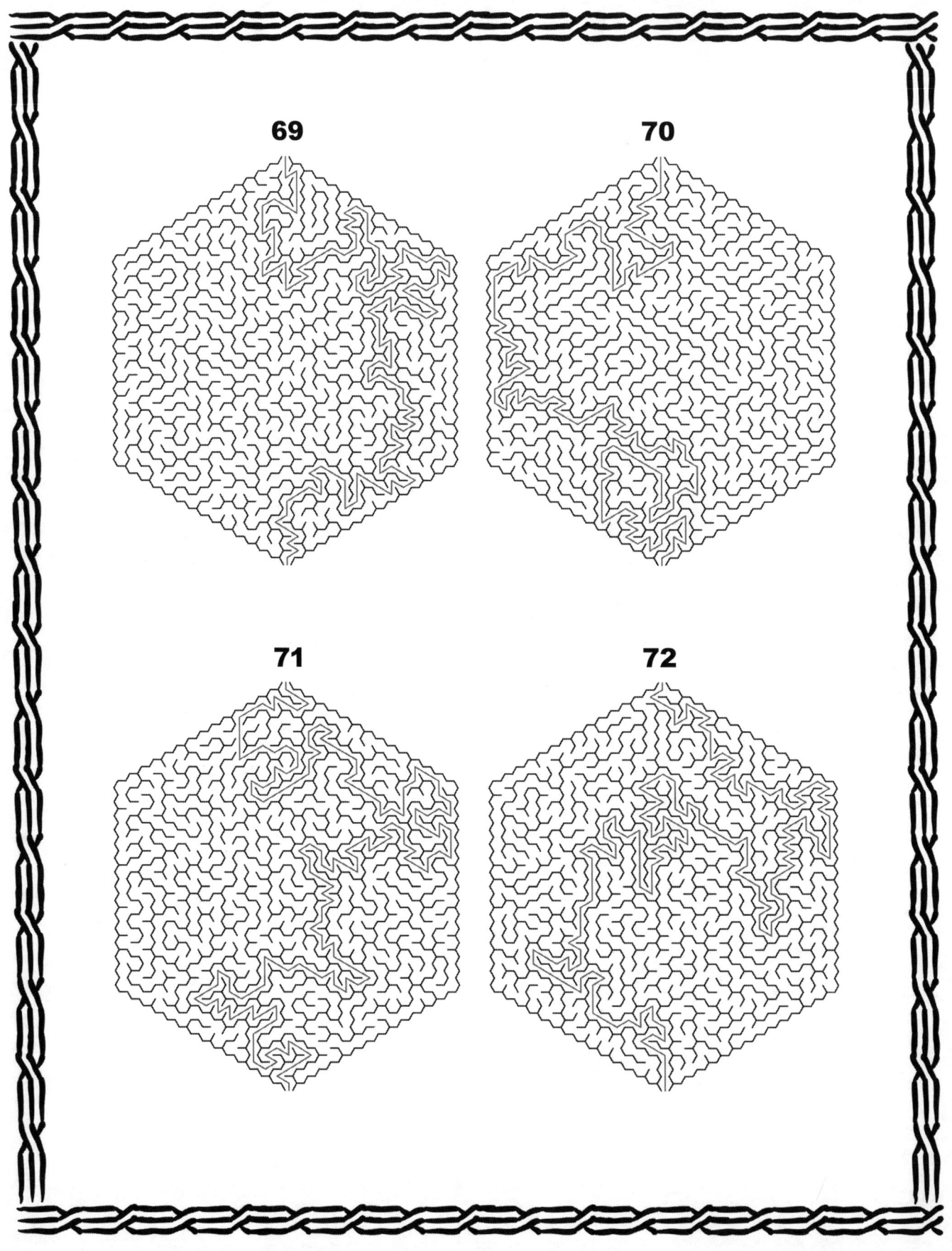

73

74

75

76

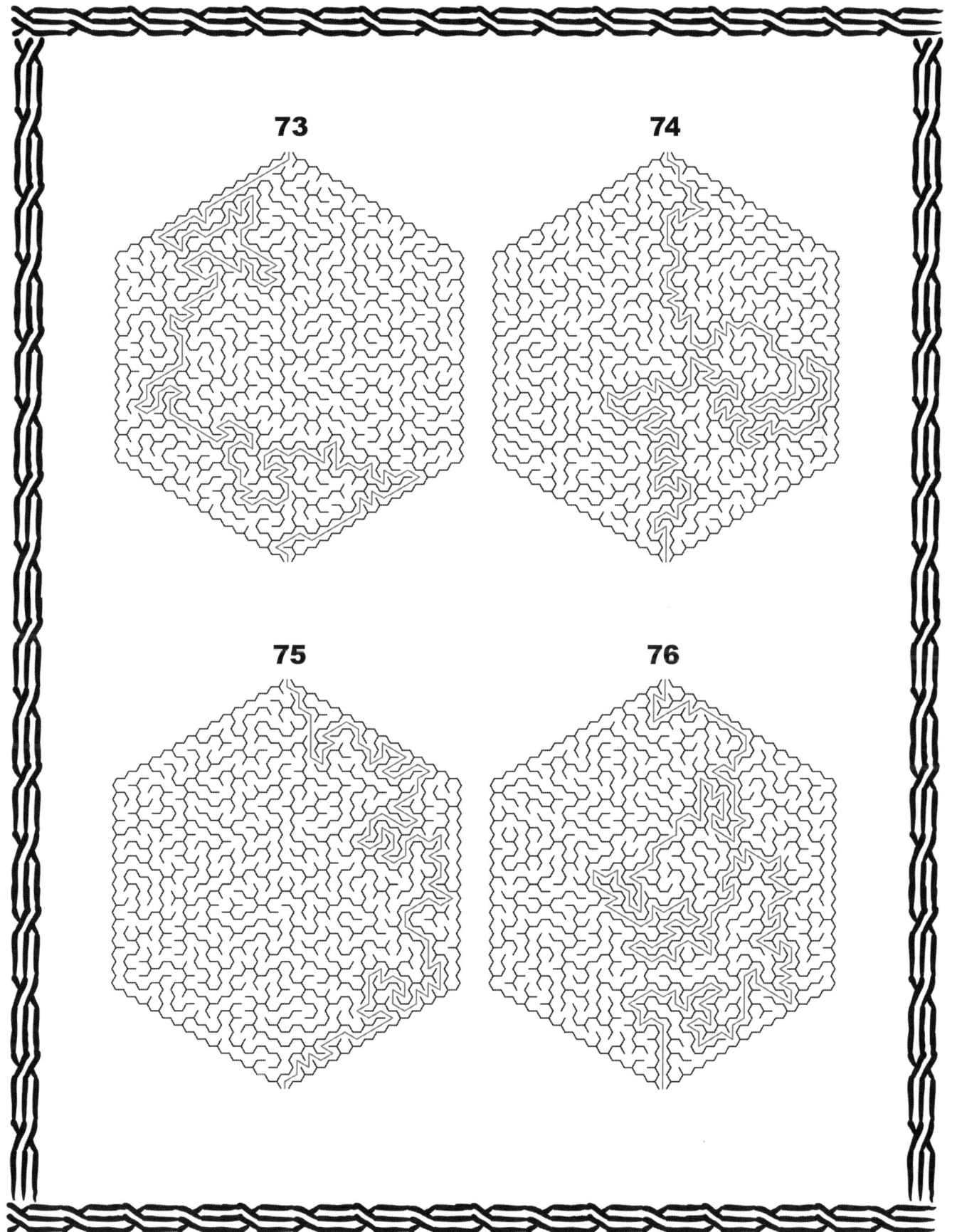

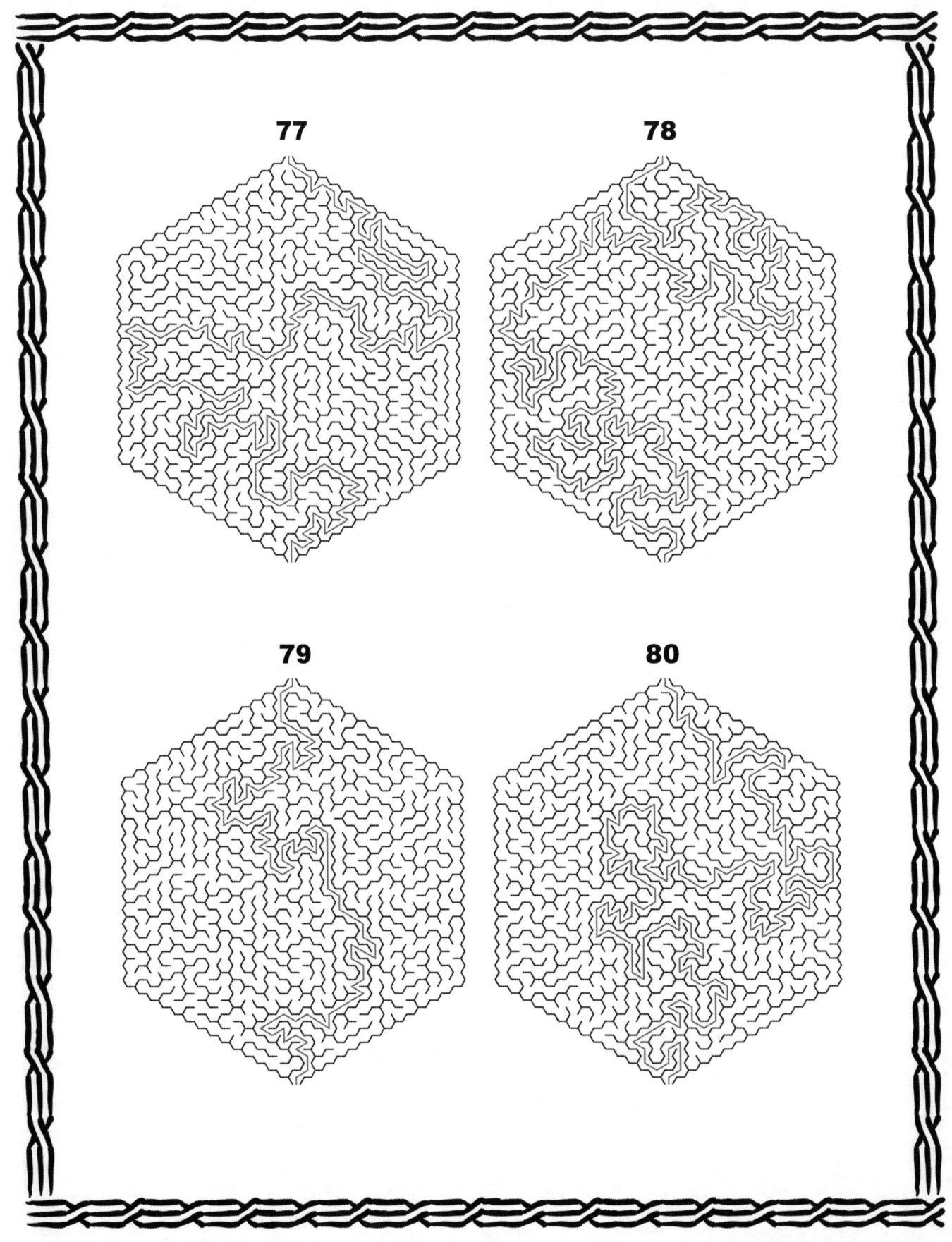

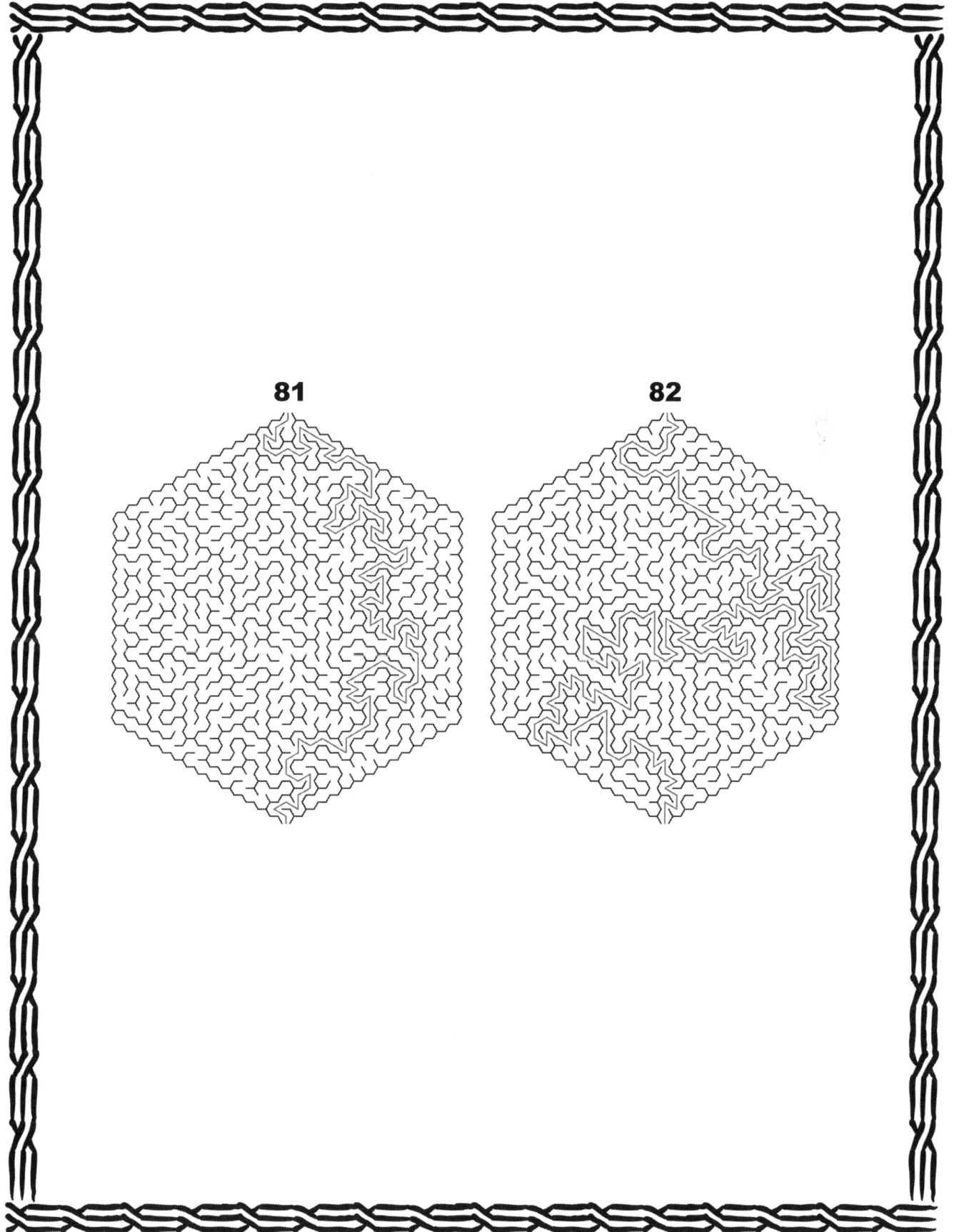

81

82

Made in the USA
Monee, IL
07 July 2026

56547354R00059